East Coasting

East Coasting

The Ultimate Roadtripper's Guide to New England

Text by Christine Chitnis
Illustrations by Monica Dorazewski

ARTISAN BOOKS | NEW YORK

Library of Congress Cataloging-in-Publication Data

Names: Chitnis, Christine, author. | Dorazewski, Monica, illustrator.
Title: East Coasting : the ultimate roadtripper's guide to New England /
    text by Christine A. Chitnis ; Illustrations by Monica Dorazewski.
Description: New York : Artisan Books, [2024]
Identifiers: LCCN 2023045266 | ISBN 9781648293184 (hardback : alk. paper)
Subjects: LCSH: Automobile travel—New England—Guidebooks. | New
    England—Description and travel.
Classification: LCC GV1024 .C57 2024 | DDC 917.404/44—dc23/eng/20231025
LC record available at https://lccn.loc.gov/2023045266

Design by Jane Treuhaft and Monica Dorazewski

Artisan books may be purchased in bulk for business, educational, or promotional use.
For information, please contact your local bookseller or the Hachette Book Group
Special Markets Department at special.markets@hbgusa.com.

The publisher is not responsible for websites (or their content) that are not owned by
the publisher.

The Hachette Speakers Bureau provides a wide range of authors for speaking
events. To find out more, go to hachettespeakersbureau.com or email
HachetteSpeakers@hbgusa.com.

Published by Artisan,
an imprint of Workman Publishing,
a division of Hachette Book Group, Inc.
1290 Avenue of the Americas
New York, NY 10104
artisanbooks.com

The Artisan name and logo are registered trademarks of Hachette Book Group, Inc.

Printed in China (APO) on responsibly sourced paper

10 9 8 7 6 5 4 3 2

To those who embrace the open road
with boundless curiosity and
an unyielding spirit of adventure

CONTENTS

INTRODUCTION 8

Connecticut
19

Rhode Island
47

Massachusetts
77

New Hampshire
119

Maine
139

AND VERMONT 171

Nova Scotia
179

BEFORE WE PART 195

ROAD TRIP SCAVENGER HUNT 196

INTRODUCTION

When I was growing up in the Midwest, my family celebrated crossing into a different state by honking the car horn, rolling down all the windows, and whooping for joy. That's what a rarity it was for us to make it out of Michigan. For the duration of my childhood, road-tripping meant going "up north," a four- to five-hour drive from Detroit to the lakes of northern Michigan. We'd pack the car full of snacks and books, load up on mixtapes, and hit the open road. Honestly, we never felt the need to leave the state, such was the grandeur of the north. In hindsight, my concept of road-tripping could more accurately be labeled day-tripping!

I often tell my children tales of growing up in Michigan, and they laugh with disbelief, both at the concept of mixtapes and the idea that crossing a state border would elicit cheers. Here in Rhode Island, where they were all born and raised, we cross over state borders several times a day. In fact, we had to disable the automatic system in our minivan that would announce "Welcome to Massachusetts" over and over again as we drove from our home to school and soccer practice.

There's something special about this region of the country, known as New England, which includes Connecticut, Rhode Island, Massachusetts, New Hampshire, Maine, and Vermont: the relatively small states, the diversity of landscapes, and the deeply rooted history of the area and its people. Having called Rhode Island home for fifteen years, I can say with certainty that the proximity to surrounding states is one of my favorite parts of this region. We can hop in the car and go antiquing in Stonington, Connecticut, or take a quick ferry ride to visit friends on Martha's Vineyard. A glorious summer day might call for a morning at Horseneck Beach in Massachusetts, and a particularly bountiful snowfall merits a trip to New Hampshire for winter sporting. My husband and I love a weekend getaway to Portland, Maine, where you can feast your way through the city, enjoying meal after fantastic meal. My son's soccer tournaments routinely take us up and down the coast, from Connecticut to New Hampshire, during the prettiest season of all, autumn, when the whole of New England is aglow with changing leaves. Living here, you always have a sense that there's something new to discover around every bend in the road.

How to Use This Book

This book features some of my favorite spots along the coast, with fun facts, historical context, and cultural touchstones peppered throughout. This certainly isn't a comprehensive guide, nor an exact map on how best to navigate from one spot to the next. Consider it a jumping-off point for planning your own unique adventure. Part of the joy of road-tripping is allowing for spontaneity, and many of the most memorable travel moments can arise from unplanned, spur-of-the-moment stops. So while a rough itinerary and a map are useful, leave room for surprises.

Many people start in Connecticut and work their way north, which is the way this book flows. However, you can jump on and off the route at whatever point suits you best. Perhaps you are leaving from Boston and heading to Halifax, or starting from Portland and heading to New York City. This book works in both cases! Just don't forget your passport, as the very northern route of this road trip includes crossing into Canada.

Because New England states are on the smaller side, especially when you narrow them down to just their coastal area, it would be easy to drive this entire route in just a few days if you were in a time crunch. But I'd encourage you to slow down and give even the tiniest state, Rhode Island, at least a few days.

Once you've decided on your route, it's time to figure out accommodations. If you prefer a rugged option, there is excellent camping to be had along the coast. Personally, I love exploring the intersection of design and hospitality, so I'm apt to seek out an independently owned bespoke hotel or inn, of which there are plenty along this route. Whatever you choose, make your reservation in advance, especially if you are traveling during the busy summer and fall seasons.

Land Acknowledgment

The land presently known as New England has long served as home to Indigenous peoples including the Abenaki, Mohegan, Mohican, Wampanoag, Munsee, Pequot, Nipmuc, Quinnipiac, Massachusett, Niantic, Pokanoket, Pennacook, and Narragansett tribes, which include the Chappaquiddick, Cowasuck, Hassanamisco, Mashpee, Mattabesic, Nulhegan, Paugussett, Pocomtuc, and Schaghticoke bands and communities.

It is thought that Indigenous people came to the New England area nine to twelve thousand years ago and lived off the land by hunting, fishing, and farming. Each community had its own distinct culture, language, and traditions. Around the 1600s, as the earliest English settlers made their way to New England, the region was home to roughly sixty thousand Native people. European colonization devastated Indigenous communities through disease, forced displacement, and violence. Many Indigenous people were killed or enslaved, and their land was taken from them. Despite the brutal campaigns against them, Indigenous communities continue to live on these lands today, keeping their cultures and traditions alive.

To honor and respect the diverse Native peoples connected to this land, there are land acknowledgment maps available, and they are worth seeking out as you travel.

Movie Night

Before you hit the open road, set the scene with these classic movies, filmed on location along the New England coastline.

Moonrise Kingdom

The Departed

Good Will Hunting

Mystic Pizza

The Cider House Rules

Jaws

Road Trip Playlist

No drive is complete without a stellar playlist of classic tunes to help melt the miles away. No matter what year you were born, or your musical taste, you'll most likely know and love the lyrics to these songs, which makes them perfect for windows-open, singing-at-the-top-of-your-lungs driving!

"Graceland"
Paul Simon

"On the Radio"
Donna Summer

"Little Red Corvette"
Prince

"Dreams"
The Cranberries

**"Into the
Great Wide Open"**
Tom Petty

"Go Your Own Way"
Fleetwood Mac

"Life Is a Highway"
Tom Cochrane

**"Dancing in the
Moonlight"**
King Harvest

"Drive"
R.E.M.

"New Sensations"
Lou Reed

"Unknown Legend"
Neil Young

"River"
Joni Mitchell

"Route 66"
The Rolling Stones

"Superstition"
Stevie Wonder

**"It Ain't Over 'til
It's Over"**
Lenny Kravitz

"Galileo"
The Indigo Girls

"Fast Car"
Tracy Chapman

"Wagon Wheel"
Old Crow Medicine Show

When to Go

While New England's coastal climate varies depending on the latitude, blustery winters and mild summers are the norm. Proximity to the Atlantic Ocean makes the region susceptible to frequent nor'easters, which can cause extreme weather. All four seasons are distinct, and each offers its own unique beauty. In spring, once the mud season has subsided, ancient magnolia and cherry trees burst into bloom. Summer's soft warmth carries with it the promise of long, lazy beach days. New England's climate has its glories, the greatest of which is the autumn foliage, when the trees transition from the verdant hues of summer to the fiery colors of fall. The days are often sunny and warm, while a chill creeps into the evening air, carrying with it a whisper of the coming winter.

Notable New England Authors

New England is synonymous with great stories. Throughout the ages New England's landscapes and people have acted as muses to some of our country's most treasured authors and poets. You can visit the homes of the following notable literary figures:

Robert Frost
(The Robert Frost Farm State Historic Site, Derry, New Hampshire)

Ralph Waldo Emerson
(The Ralph Waldo Emerson House, Concord, Massachusetts)

Harriet Beecher Stowe
(Harriet Beecher Stowe Center, Hartford, Connecticut)

Emily Dickinson
(The Homestead & the Evergreens, Amherst, Massachusetts)

Mark Twain
(The Mark Twain House & Museum, Hartford, Connecticut)

Louisa May Alcott
(Orchard House, Concord, Massachusetts)

What to Bring

A well-packed vehicle can make all the difference when it comes to road-tripping, and here are a few ideas to get you started. Weather can change quickly in New England, so pack a variety of layers and different footwear. Don't forget your passport, as we'll be crossing into Canada!

Foldable sun hat

Phone charger

Bug spray

Sunscreen

Sketchbook and pencils

Raincoat

Quick-drying towel

Sweater

Travel shampoo, conditioner, and bodywash

Waterproof beach blanket

Water bottle

Snacks

Large tote

Utensils

Candle and matches

Fishing pole

Sunglasses

Water shoes

Rain boots

CONNECTICUT

—

the
Constitution
State

WELCOME TO

Connecticut

From Mystic's picturesque harbor to Norwalk's beautiful beaches, Connecticut's shore is a place of unending charm. Summers here are dreamy: long days at the beach, ocean waves gently lapping at the shore; fresh-caught seafood paired with the plentiful delights of the region's many farm stands and farmers markets. As the joke goes, if you can't afford a house on the ocean, make friends with someone who can! Some of my fondest memories of the Connecticut coast include visiting friends in Stonington. We spent our days shuttling from beach to beach in their tiny skiff, stopping for steamers and lobster rolls at a clapboard shack on stilts that jutted out into the sea. Connecticut's coastline is home to some of the most beautiful beaches in New England, from the tranquil waters of Silver Sands State Park to the rolling waves of Hammonasset Beach State Park. With sand between our toes and a sea breeze in our hair, those carefree summer days felt endless.

Within its compact borders, the Constitution State offers so much more than dazzling beaches. You'll find forested hills, bustling cityscapes, and historic villages, as well as a prestigious Ivy League school (Yale) and a diverse landscape of cultural, historic, and artistic touchstones. The region's rich maritime history is on full display in museums, lighthouses, and historic landmarks. Learn about the history of whaling and shipbuilding at the Mystic Seaport Museum, or visit the state's oldest and tallest lighthouse, New London Harbor Lighthouse. History buffs will take great pleasure in exploring Connecticut's important role in the American Revolution: providing food, supplies, and ammunition to the soldiers. There are numerous historical monuments and sites that commemorate the state's contributions to the war effort, including Fort Griswold Battlefield State Park in Groton and the Soldiers' and Sailors' Monument in New Haven.

While Connecticut achieved statehood in 1788, the Native peoples, including the Pequots, Mohegans, Paugussetts, and Schaghticokes, called the land home for more than ten thousand years before European fishermen, travelers, and traders began arriving in the 1600s. Although it requires a slight detour from the coast, pay a visit to the Mashantucket Pequot Museum and the Tantaquidgeon Museum, the oldest tribally owned and operated museum in the United States, to learn about the history and present-day life of the Pequots and Mohegans.

the Charles W. Morgan,
Mystic Seaport Museum

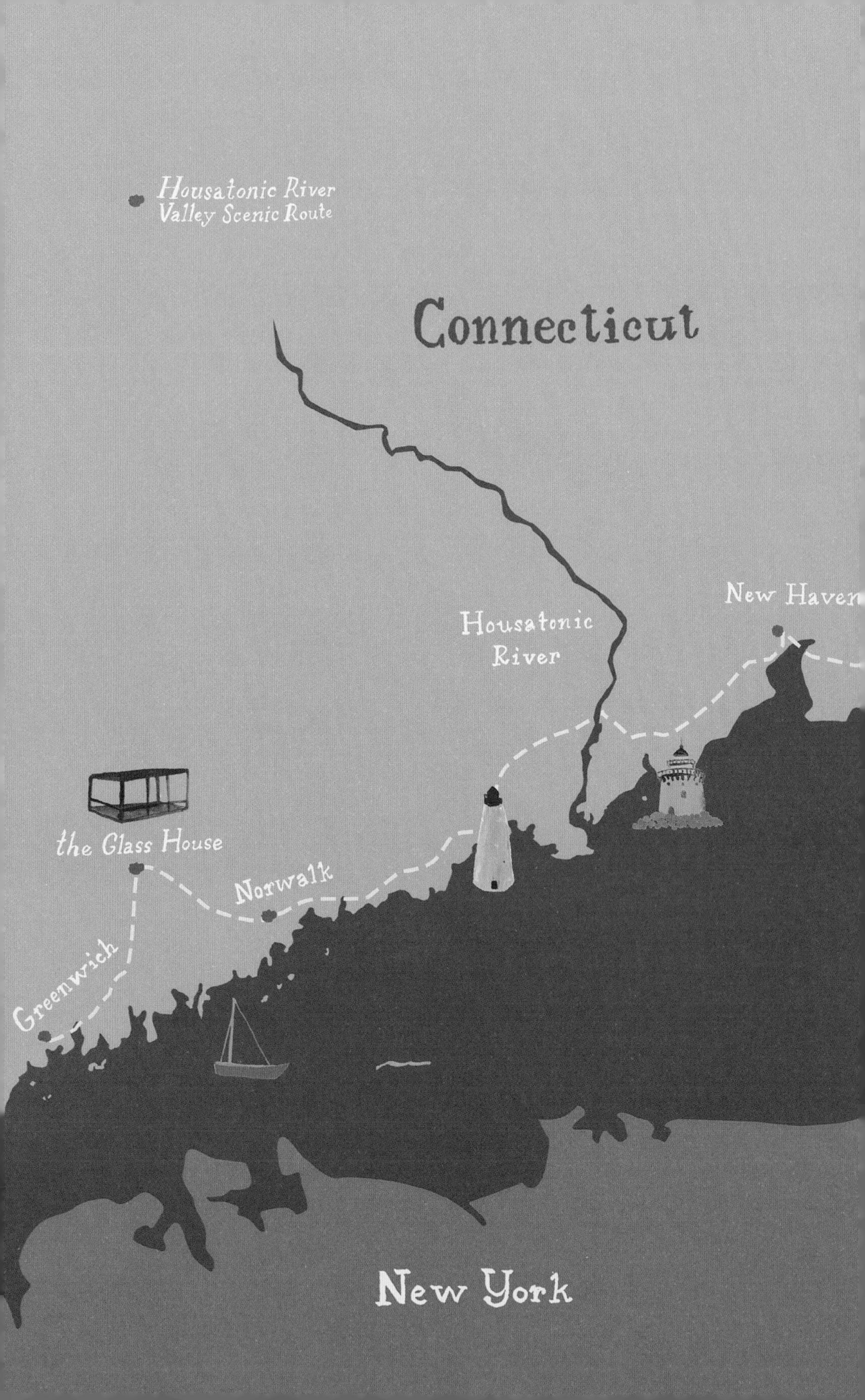

Housatonic River
Valley Scenic Route

Connecticut

New Haven

Housatonic
River

the Glass House

Norwalk

Greenwich

New York

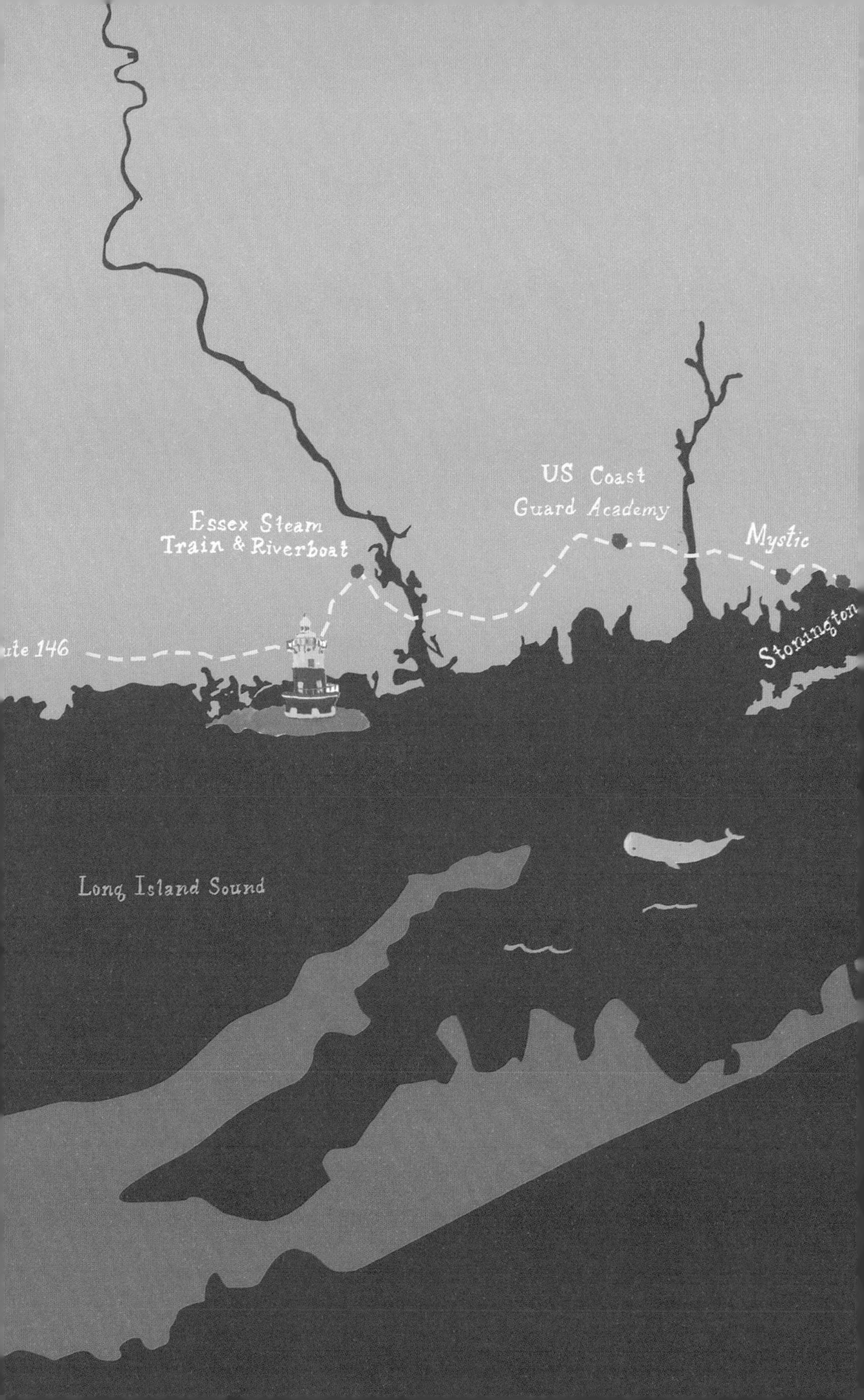

US Coast
Guard Academy

Essex Steam
Train & Riverboat

Mystic

ute 146

Stonington

Long Island Sound

Sheffield Island Light

DESTINATIONS

Greenwich
26

Norwalk
28

The Glass House
30

New Haven
35

Essex Steam Train & Riverboat
38

Mystic
41

Stonington
42

GREENWICH

From New York City, take I-95 north for 35 miles to Greenwich. Established in 1640, this beautiful, affluent town is one of the oldest in Connecticut. Greenwich is known for its extravagant homes, and you can get a peek at some by driving through the neighborhoods of Old Greenwich, Riverside, and Belle Haven, which overlook the waterfront. Belle Haven is close to downtown, where you can stroll down **Greenwich Avenue** and enjoy the upscale shops and restaurants. Book lovers will want to make a stop at **Diane's Books**, a popular independent bookstore.

For a small town, Greenwich offers impressive historical and cultural touchstones. Visit the newly renovated, strikingly modern **Bruce Museum**, a community-based art and science institution that features a diverse array of exhibitions and collections, ranging from fine art and natural science specimens to cultural artifacts and interactive educational displays. The Bruce is just one stop on the

Bruce Museum

Greenwich Polo Club

Connecticut Art Trail, which includes twenty-three world-class museums and historical sites (farms, art studios, and former artists' boardinghouses) and spans multiple genres—from European masterpieces and modern art to ancient art and contemporary culture. Just 2 miles down the road, the **Bush-Holley House** offers an opportunity to step back in time and experience the birthplace of American impressionism. The house and grounds served as an artist colony in the late 1800s and early 1900s, when Greenwich's bucolic landscapes—bustling harbors, tidal wetlands, meandering rivers, wooded creeks, and stone walls—were a draw for plein air artists seeking inspiration. Today, the house is a museum showcasing the work of the artists who lived there, as well as the cultural and social influences that shaped their art.

If you're in town during the summer months, be sure to catch a fast-paced, elegant polo match at the **Greenwich Polo Club**. The club hosts tournaments and events featuring some of the world's top players.

NORWALK

About 12 miles north of Greenwich sits **Rowayton**, a tiny coastal village within the city limits of Norwalk. Bordered by Long Island Sound to the south and east and the Five Mile River to the west, the peninsula has a rich oystering and lobstering history. The village is mostly residential (the downtown spans less than half a mile), but the beaches—particularly **Bayley Beach**, with its playground, pavilion, and kayak launch—and the 16-acre **Farm Creek Preserve** are a big draw.

Five miles from Rowayton, you'll hit Norwalk. Start your journey by visiting the **Maritime Aquarium**, home to more than seventy-five exhibits comprising 2,700 marine animals from around the world, including seals, jellyfish, and penguins. Take a stroll through the beautiful **Oyster Shell Park**, where scenic walking paths and bird-watching areas offer clear views of Long Island Sound. A coastal community at heart, Norwalk offers plentiful beaches; favorites include **Calf Pasture Beach** and **Shady Beach**. For a dose of maritime history, visit the **Sheffield Island Light**, a lighthouse built in 1868 and open seasonally for tours.

Delve into the city's affluent history at the **Lockwood-Mathews Mansion Museum**. This impressive Victorian-era mansion built for the railroad and banking magnate LeGrand Lockwood embodies the opulent lifestyle of the nineteenth-century elite. The **Center for Contemporary Printmaking**, a nonprofit organization dedicated to promoting the art of printmaking through exhibitions, education, and outreach programs, is worth a stop. Browse the exhibits or sign up for a workshop. End your day with a visit to the vibrant **South Norwalk (SoNo) Historic District**, where you'll find a range of restaurants, bars, and shops.

Antiquing in New England

Antiquing in coastal New England offers a journey back through history, inviting collectors to unearth hidden treasures. The region's rich maritime heritage and colonial past provide a unique backdrop for discovering vintage nautical artifacts and well-preserved estate heirlooms.

THE GLASS HOUSE

Just a quick drive from Norwalk, New Canaan's **Glass House**, designed by Philip Johnson and completed in 1949, is a regional jewel. Johnson was an American architect whose modern and postmodern works, including the Glass House and the Sculpture Garden of New York's Museum of Modern Art, are widely considered masterpieces of the twentieth century. With its glass-walled rooms, the striking Glass House has become an iconic symbol of mid-century modern design—and is now owned by the National Trust for Historic Preservation. The estate also includes fourteen other structures designed by Johnson, including the Brick House, Painting Gallery, Sculpture Gallery, Pavilion in the Pond, and Ghost House. Guided tours begin at the visitor center (199 Elm Street). Tickets are required for admission, and the house closes during the winter months.

New Canaan is well known for its architectural heritage. **Tirranna** (aka the Rayward-Shepherd House), designed in 1955 by Frank Lloyd Wright, is another notable architectural landmark in New Canaan, though it is a private property and not open to the public.

HOUSATONIC RIVER VALLEY SCENIC ROUTE

From New Canaan, the Housatonic River Valley Scenic Route (US 7) offers a worthwhile detour, especially during fall, when the hills framing the river blaze with color. The rustic two-lane byway, which runs about 25 miles, crosses its namesake river twice and winds through **Kent Falls State Park** and **Housatonic Meadows State Park**. You'll also pass within sight of the iconic 1864 **West Cornwall Covered Bridge**.

West Cornwall Covered Bridge

Kent Falls State Park

Housatonic Meadows State Park

Yale Peabody Museum

NEW HAVEN

CT 8 offers the most straightforward route back to the coast, to New Haven, founded in 1638 and now known as the cultural capital of Connecticut thanks to its plethora of theaters, museums, nightlife, restaurants, and musical venues, as well as the presence of Yale University. Start your day on the Yale campus, specifically at the **Yale Peabody Museum**. The museum has a vast collection of natural history specimens, including dinosaur fossils, meteorites, and Egyptian mummies. Be sure to check out the Great Hall of Dinosaurs and the Hall of Minerals, Earth, and Space. After the museum, head to the **Yale University Art Gallery**, which has an extensive collection of art from around the world. Admission to the museum is free. Other Yale historic buildings include **Harkness Tower**, **Sterling Memorial Library**, and the **Beinecke Rare Book & Manuscript Library**, one of the world's largest libraries devoted entirely to rare books and manuscripts.

For lunch, "apizza" is a must. What cheesesteaks are to Philly, apizza is to New Haven. The "a" is a nod to the Italian dialect spoken in the Naples region and New Haven's history as a town of Italian immigrants. Visit **Frank Pepe Pizzeria Napoletana**, known as Pepe's, which was the first pizzeria to open on Wooster Street in 1925, followed by the equally adored **Sally's Apizza** in 1938. Both are known for their thin-crust pizzas, brought to a char as they cook over coals.

After fueling up, head to **West Rock Ridge State Park**, located a few miles outside of downtown New Haven. With 21 miles of hiking trails and mountain biking, the park offers distant views of New Haven Harbor and Long Island Sound from atop West Rock, the large traprock the park was named after. Within the park, visit **Judges Cave**, a historic site where two judges, Edward Whalley and William Goffe, hid after signing the death warrant of King Charles I of England.

The Ivy League

Out of the eight prestigious Ivy League universities, four are located in New England: Yale, Harvard, Brown, and Dartmouth. With sprawling, majestic campuses, beautifully manicured green spaces, rich histories, and engaged student bodies, these institutions bear visiting, whether you are a prospective student or curious interloper. Fun fact: Known simply as "the Game," the annual football match between Harvard and Yale perpetuates the second-oldest continuing rivalry in college football, with the first competition having taken place in New Haven in 1875. (Yale also holds the record for the oldest rivalry in college football—with Princeton.)

→ ROUTE 146 SCENIC DRIVE

Just outside of New Haven, you'll come to **Branford**, one of Connecticut's many shoreline towns known for its marina and beaches. Look for the signs to **Route 146 Scenic Drive**, a 12-mile detour through a coastal landscape of salt marshes and forest that offers stunning views of the **Thimble Islands**.

ESSEX STEAM TRAIN & RIVERBOAT

Heading north along the shore, about 20 miles from Branford, you can hop aboard the **Essex Steam Train & Riverboat** to learn about the rich history of steam power and the vibrant ecology of the Connecticut River. Choose from several options, including a two-and-a-half-hour train and riverboat tour, a one-hour train ride, and a dinner train experience. No matter which journey you embark on, all rides depart from the 1892 Essex Station and journey through the nostalgic New England towns of Deep River and Chester, and past the tidal wetlands of Selden Neck State Park, Pratt Cove, and Chester Creek.

For a truly special evening, indulge in the four-course meal served on the dinner train (restored 1920s Pullman diners pulled by a vintage diesel locomotive). All aboard!

United States Coast Guard Academy

From Essex, head about 20 miles in the direction of New London. Located on the Thames River, the **United States Coast Guard Academy** is an active military installation, so while visitors are allowed, make sure you schedule your visit in advance and bring a valid photo ID. The guided tour, led by a current cadet, takes you through the beautiful campus that includes historic buildings, a chapel, and athletic facilities, and you'll get a glimpse at what life is like for cadets. Don't miss the USCG Museum, which features captivating exhibits on the history of the Coast Guard and its contributions to our country: maritime security and law enforcement, as well as search and rescue efforts. From here, Mystic is a short 10-mile drive.

MYSTIC

The town of Mystic, originally settled as a shipbuilding port in the mid-seventeenth century, is famous for its tall masts that embody the town's essence. You can experience these up close at the **Mystic Seaport Museum**, which features historic ships like the *Charles W. Morgan*—the oldest commercial ship in the United States, dating back to 1841—and a reproduction of the *Amistad* schooner. Don't miss the 1800s seaport village re-creation and the working ship-yard, where meticulous restoration takes place including of the *Mayflower II*, a replica of the *Mayflower* that is part of the Plimoth Patuxet Museums in Plymouth, Massachusetts. If you feel inspired to take your own seafaring adventure, the schooner *Argia* offers day or sunset cruises from May 1 through mid-October. Get to know what's under the sea at the **Mystic Aquarium**, recognized by the American Humane Conservation program for its renowned beluga whale rescue and rehabilitation program. You can also visit the diverse array of marine creatures, including penguins, sea lions, sharks, and rays.

Mystic is best known for its maritime history, but a close second is its famed appearance in the 1988 Julia Roberts rom-com *Mystic Pizza*. You can visit the original **Mystic Pizza** downtown, and then pop over to **Bank Square Books**. From there, walk over to the **Mystic Museum of Art**, established in 1913 by a group of New England artists led by American impressionist painter Charles H. Davis and inspired by the landscapes of nineteenth-century French painters. It is home to a permanent collection of works from the nineteenth to twenty-first centuries, spanning styles from neoclassicism to impressionism to deconstructivism.

STONINGTON

Just 5 miles from Mystic, Stonington is often voted one of the prettiest coastal towns in New England. Its historic downtown is filled with colonial-era homes, quaint storefronts, and cobblestone streets. Its picturesque harbor was once a hub for whaling and fishing activities, and today it's home to Connecticut's last remaining fishing and lobstering fleets. To learn more about the area's maritime history, visit the **Captain Nathaniel B. Palmer House Museum**, which features a collection of exhibits and artifacts that highlight the town's role in the whaling industry and the story of "Captain Nat," who was an American sealing captain. Set aside time to poke around the many restaurants, shops, and antiques markets along **Water Street**. Owned by avid sailors, the **Dog Watch Café** overlooks the harbor and is the perfect spot to grab a bite and watch the boats come in. Located at the southernmost tip of Water Street, **duBois Beach** provides calm swimming waters and fantastic views of Stonington Harbor, Fishers Island Sound, and Little Narragansett Bay.

Roseate
Tern

Peregrine
Falcon

Shorebirds of Barn Island Wildlife Management Area in Stonington

This 1,013-acre shoreline tract is the state's single largest coastal property managed for wildlife conservation, and the 5.3-mile trail is perfect for birders. Weaving through fields, forests, and salt marsh landscapes, you'll spot a diverse array of avian species. Here are a few to get you started.

Saltmarsh
Sparrow

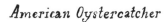

American Oystercatcher

Piping Plover

New England Produce
THROUGH THE SEASONS

The bright, bracing flavors of spring's produce signal the end of a long New England winter. And soon after the first tender shoots appear, we're awash in peas, asparagus, radishes, and greens. From there, the abundance of summer and fall displays the region's robust local farm-fresh offerings. Swing by a roadside market, seek out a farmers market, or visit a farm and pick your own!

SPRING

Asparagus • Strawberries • Snow peas •
Spring onions • Rhubarb • Fiddlehead ferns

SUMMER

Plums • Blueberries • Peaches • Zucchini •
Cucumbers • Tomatoes • Corn • Eggplant •
Raspberries • Watermelon

FALL

Butternut squash • Brussels sprouts • Pumpkin •
Pears • Cranberries • Apples • Fennel • Parsnips

RHODE ISLAND

the Ocean State

Rhode Island

With 400 miles of Atlantic shoreline, the tiny state of Rhode Island packs more beauty within its borders than almost any other coastal destination. The Ocean State is known for hardworking harbor towns, fresh seafood, lovely beaches, and quintessential New England allure. Summertime here is beautiful, and the miles of coastline offer something for every kind of beach enthusiast: surfing, family-friendly spots, bird-watching, or peace and quiet. Don't miss Little Rhody summer staples like clam cakes; Del's frozen lemonade; coffee milk; and doughboys—deep-fried, sugar-dusted confections available at almost every beach stand. But there's so much more to dive into than just surf, sand, and snacks. When the tourists vanish and the leaves begin to turn, the real charms of the state's bucolic small towns—Warren, Bristol, Tiverton, Little Compton, and Westerly, to name a few—are revealed through the quiet hush, golden meadows, verdant vineyards, shingled farmhouses, and striking crisp blue of Narragansett Bay.

It's important to note that although it is nearly surrounded by water, Rhode Island is not an island! I know, it is unnecessarily confusing. To get around here, you will be passing over many bridges that take you to all the various coastal towns, many of which are actually located on islands off the main shore. Newport and Middletown, for example, are on Aquidneck Island, while Jamestown is situated on Conanicut Island. For a true island experience that can't be reached by bridge, take a quick 12-mile ferry ride to Block Island, a fishing and farming community that also serves as a pastoral, peaceful summer vacation spot. It's safe to say that no matter where you go in Rhode Island, you're never more than a stone's throw from the sea.

Having lived in Providence for the past fifteen years, I'm biased in my love for the creative capital city, which was founded by Roger Williams in 1636, more than a century before the founding of the country. With exceptional food, neoclassical architecture, an engaging art scene, and a handful of renowned colleges and universities—including the Rhode Island School of Design and Brown University—the city, though impressive, remains unpretentious and funky. Wander through College Hill's leafy streets, paved with crooked cobblestones, and marvel at the stately historic homes, many of which date back to the eighteenth century. The Providence River runs through downtown, and on designated nights throughout the summer and fall months, bonfires are lit on the river as gondolas float downstream and the city celebrates WaterFire, equal parts public art and street party. There's always intriguing street art to explore, and the murals throughout downtown give a nod to the diverse communities that make up our great state.

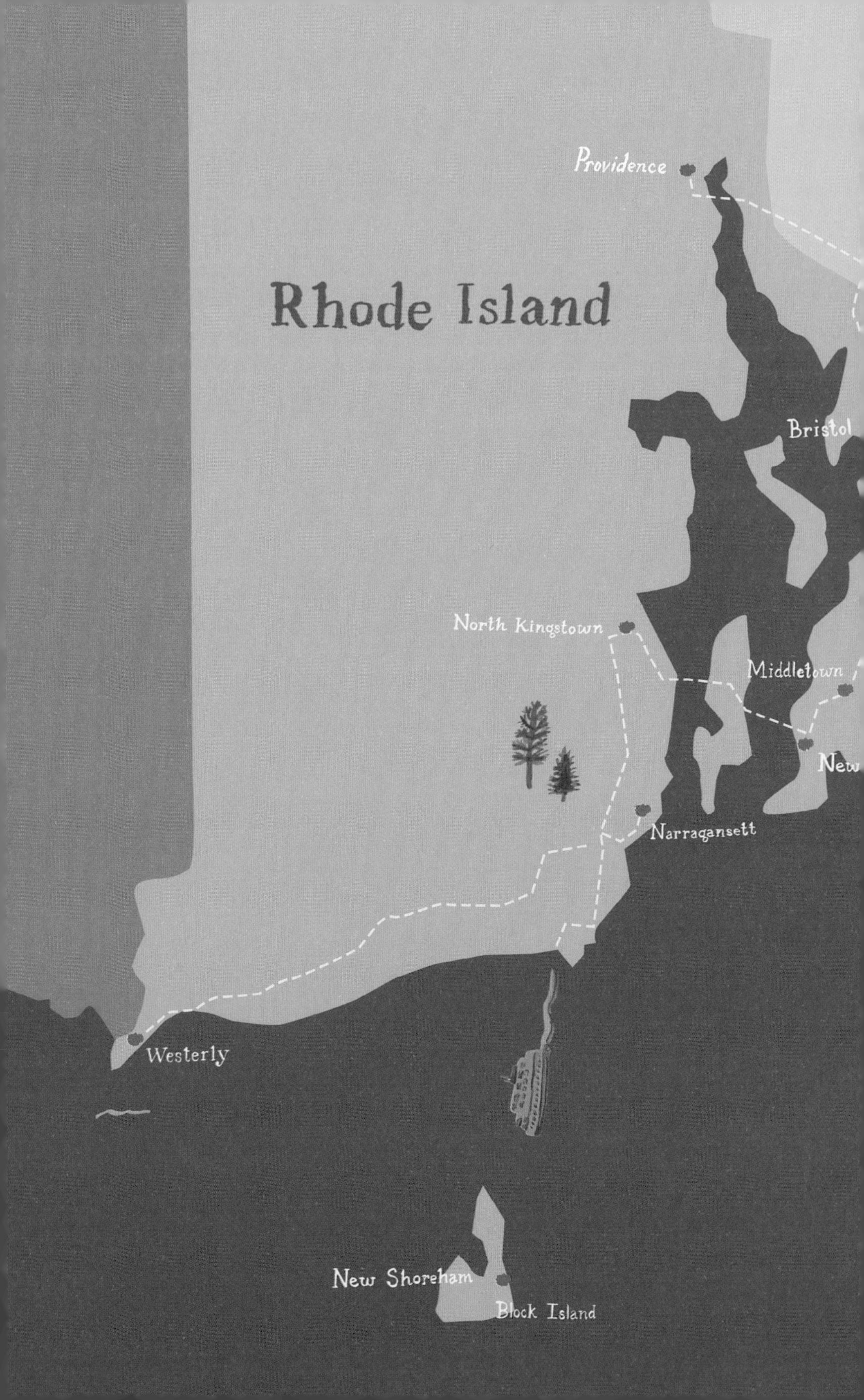

Rhode Island

Providence

Bristol

North Kingstown

Middletown

New

Narragansett

Westerly

New Shoreham

Block Island

Massachusetts

DESTINATIONS

Watch Hill
54

Narragansett
57

North Kingstown
(and Route 1A)
59

Newport
62

Middletown
66

The Farm Coast
68

Bristol
70

Providence
72

WATCH HILL

From Stonington, Connecticut, you'll curve around the Barn Island Wildlife Management Area and cross into Rhode Island. It's a scant 10-mile trip. Located on the southernmost tip of the state, Watch Hill is part of the larger town of Westerly and beloved for its stunning, sizable homes and beaches. As you drive in on Watch Hill Road, the sunny yellow grand facade of **Ocean House**, a historic luxury hotel with an outstanding food and wine program, appears on the horizon. Park your car wherever you can find a spot, because from here, the lovely streets of Watch Hill are easily walkable. Spend the day enjoying the sun and surf at **Watch Hill Beach**, or opt for a more active experience at **Napatree Point Conservation Area**, which serves as a wildlife preserve and home to nesting migratory birds. If you hike around the peninsula, you can expect to cover close to 4 miles.

Back in Watch Hill, take a ride on the **Flying Horse Carousel**, one of the oldest working carousels in the country, believed to have been built around 1876. Unlike with most modern carousels, the horses are not attached to the platform but rather suspended by chains. Centrifugal force drives the horses outward, causing them to "fly." It's a hit with kids of all ages. In the middle of the ride, a device holding metal rings is lowered for riders to grab as they pass. Try to grab the golden ring to win a free ride! Nearby, don't miss **Misquamicut State Beach** and **East Beach**.

Flying Horse Carousel

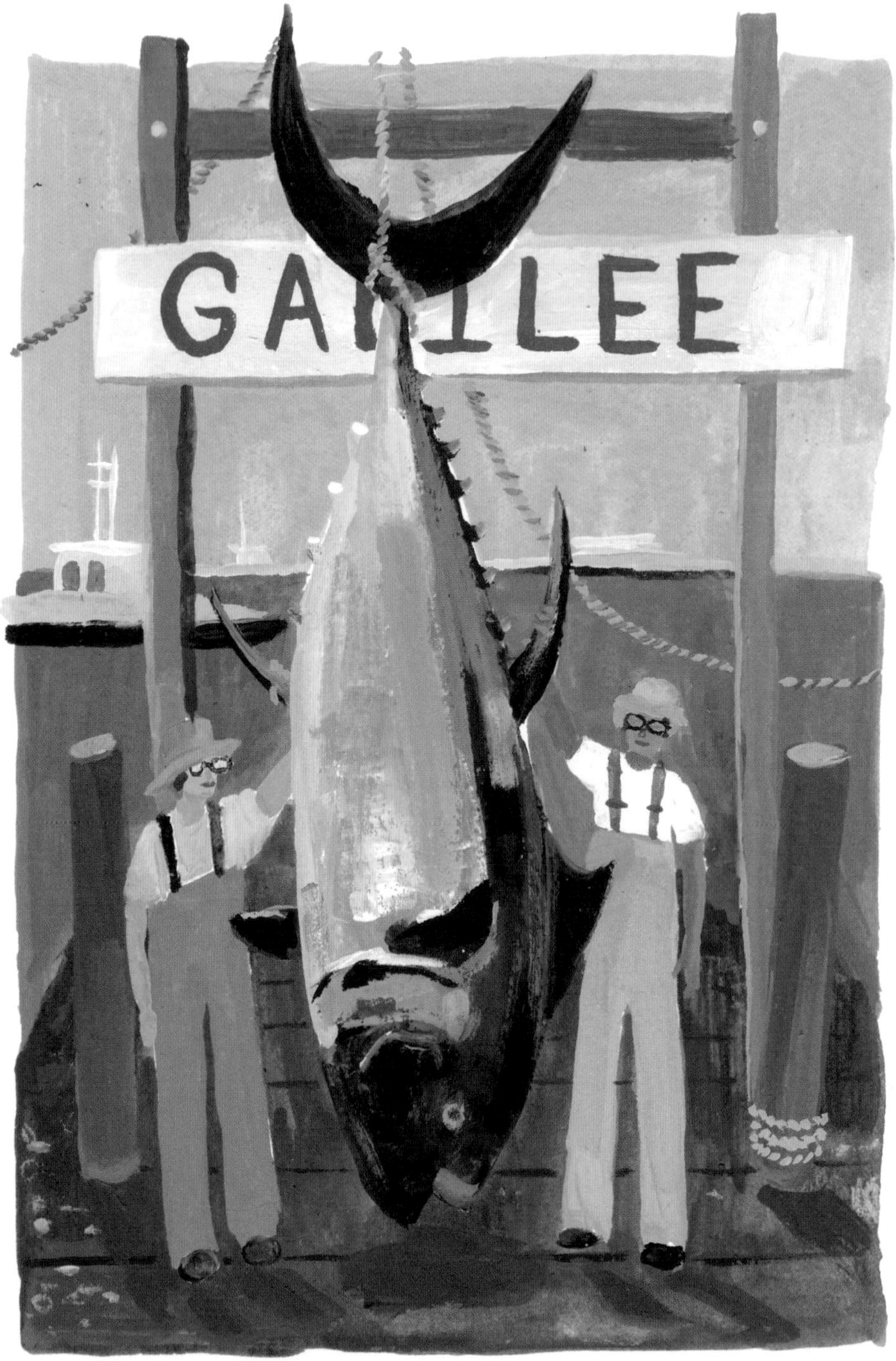
GA ILEE

NARRAGANSETT

Take Route 1 from Westerly to Narragansett, weaving through Weekapaug, Quonochontaug, and Charlestown, and don't hesitate to pull off and explore the beautiful coastal ponds and shoreline. Carve out some time to slurp oysters at the renowned waterfront restaurant **Matunuck Oyster Bar**, which serves delicious seafood dishes made from locally sourced ingredients.

The town is named after the Narragansett people. Engage with the state's Indigenous culture and arts, both historic and contemporary, with a visit to the **Tomaquag Museum**, which is operated by the Narragansett tribe and is Rhode Island's only museum dedicated to telling the story of the state's first people from an Indigenous perspective.

Narragansett is known for its beaches, and the obvious favorite is **Narragansett Town Beach**, located in the center of town. The beach officially opens on Memorial Day weekend, and from that point on, around five thousand beachgoers a day crowd the shores. Perhaps you can see why those who live in the area love the shoulder seasons of spring and fall, when the beaches are crowd-free, the water is a bit chilly, and the waves are perfect for surfing. Other Narragansett beaches include **Scarborough State Beaches**, **Roger W. Wheeler State Beach**, and **Salty Brine State Beach**. To learn more about Rhode Island's rich coastal legacy, including the commercial fishing industry, visit the **South County Museum**, which explores local history through artifacts, memorabilia, and hands-on exhibits. Take a stroll through the working fishing village of **Galilee**, one of the most productive commercial fishing ports on the East Coast. The tiny village boasts more than ten seafood restaurants, and fresh lobster and fish are available to purchase right off the docks. This is the best place to catch the Block Island Ferry, which will get you to the island in under an hour.

→ BLOCK ISLAND

Only 9 miles off the coast, Block Island makes a perfect day-trip destination, with gorgeous beaches and bucolic scenery. The shortest ferry ride is from Point Judith in Galilee, but you can also catch a ferry from Newport; Fall River, Massachusetts; New London, Connecticut; and Montauk, New York. At only 7 miles across and 3 miles wide, the island is best covered by bike. The self-guided bike tour runs about 16 miles and is quite hilly, but the views are not to be missed! Along the route, stop at **Mansion Beach**, the **Clay Head Nature Trail**, the **Mohegan Bluffs**, **Rodman's Hollow**, and **Great Salt Pond**. Migratory birds spend summers here on the island, so pack a pair of binoculars and get your birding on at the **Block Island National Wildlife Refuge**. The island features two lighthouses: the **North Light**, built in 1867, at the northern tip, and the **Southeast Light**, built in 1875, at— you guessed it—the southern tip. Grab a seafood dinner at one of the restaurants in town before jumping aboard the last ferry to the mainland.

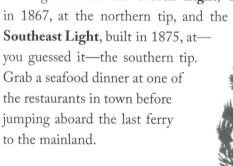

NORTH KINGSTOWN
(AND ROUTE 1A)

Start your day with a visit to the historic **Wickford Village**, one of the oldest preserved colonial-era villages in the country, where you can easily spend an afternoon browsing the eclectic shops. It is worth taking the self-guided **Historic Walking Tour** to learn more about the village's fascinating maritime history. Take Route 1A out of town—be on the lookout for a smattering of great antiques shops—and head over to **Casey Farm**, a beautiful 300-year-old farm that is still operating and open to the public. Here you can learn about the history of farming in Rhode Island and get your hands dirty helping with the harvest and participating in a variety of farm activities. On the weekends, Casey Farm hosts a farmers market, and they also offer organic vegetables, herbs, and flowers to their community-supported agriculture (CSA) subscribers.

Casey Farm

Rhode Island Lighthouses

Rhode Island boasts twenty-one working lighthouses, including the Ida Lewis Lighthouse, named after one of the most famous lighthouse keepers in history, Idawalley Zoradia Lewis. Over the course of her career, which started when she was fifteen and her father, originally appointed to the job, suffered a stroke, Lewis rescued at least eighteen people from the waters of Newport Harbor. The press anointed her the "Bravest Woman in America."

North Light
(Block Island)

Ida Lewis Lighthouse
(Newport)

Castle Hill Light
(Newport)

Point Judith Lighthouse
(Narragansett)

Plum Beach Lighthouse
(North Kingstown)

Prudence Island Lighthouse
(Prudence Island)

Sakonnet Lighthouse
(Little Compton)

NEWPORT

From North Kingstown, pass over the Jamestown Verrazzano Bridge to reach **Jamestown**, a historic small town situated on Conanicut Island. Walk around the harbor, pop into some shops, and drive around the island. It's small but bears exploring. Grab a bite at **Village Hearth Bakery & Cafe**, take a drive to **Beavertail Lighthouse Museum** on the island's southernmost tip, and load up on produce at **Watson Farm**.

Continue over the Claiborne Pell Bridge, a stunning suspension bridge that stretches across Narragansett Bay's East Passage to Newport, located on Aquidneck Island. Newport is best known as a summer destination for the rich; much of its early wealth was a result of its role as the hub of New England's slave trade, with enslaved people accounting for one-fifth of Newport's population at its height. Within Newport's Common Burying Ground, visit **God's Little Acre**, a historically noteworthy burying ground on Farewell Street that has been recognized as having possibly the oldest and largest surviving collection of grave markers of enslaved and free Africans.

Newport's reputation as a summer playground for the country's wealthiest families dates back to the late nineteenth century, the Gilded Age, when American titans of industry—including the Vanderbilts, Astors, and Morgans—flocked to its shores to build their summer "cottages," otherwise known as mansions. To understand the area's appeal, take a scenic drive along the **Ocean Drive Historic District** to enjoy breathtaking views of the Atlantic Ocean and gawk at the affluent summer homes, or stroll the 3.5-mile **Cliff Walk**, which passes by several mansions and offers stunning views of the coast. Then head to the **Newport Art Museum**, founded in 1912 and featuring the work of notable New England artists, including George Bellows, Mary Cassatt, and Childe Hassam. And don't miss visiting the **International Tennis Hall of Fame** and the **National Museum of American Illustration**, home to one of the largest collections of acclaimed American pictorial art, housed in a historic château.

The town's beaches are perfect for relaxing, soaking up some sun, and even surfing; and make sure to explore the cute, if not somewhat touristy, downtown area, where you'll find shops, galleries, and restaurants. Newport is famous in the sailing world for hosting the **America's Cup**, so take advantage of the opportunity to sail or book a boat tour of the harbor. If you happen to be in town during the last weekend of July, don't miss the annual **Newport Folk Festival** at Fort Adams, which has hosted country and folk music legends including Bob Dylan, Joni Mitchell, the Indigo Girls, James Taylor, Johnny Cash, Mavis Staples, Dolly Parton, and more. Tickets sell out fast, and in advance, so mark your calendar for on-sale dates.

Claiborne Pell Bridge

Newport Mansions

During the Gilded Age, wealthy families flocked to Newport, where they built astonishingly lavish summer homes that now serve as museums. Plan your visit and purchase tickets through the Preservation Society of Newport County.

Belcourt of Newport
Lavish former summer home completed in 1894 in the Châteauesque style, with tours by reservation

Rough Point
Late-1800s mansion formerly owned by heiress Doris Duke with gardens, art exhibits, and seasonal tours

The Elms

Gilded Age mansion featuring tours of the servants' quarters and Colonial Revival gardens

Rosecliff

Featured in the 1974 film *The Great Gatsby*, a Gilded Age mansion offering audio tours and a gift shop

The Breakers

Gilded Age mansion completed in 1895 that reflects the unimaginable wealth of the Vanderbilt family

Green Animals Topiary Garden

Featuring eighty topiary creations crafted from California privet, yew, and English boxwood, some of which originated a century ago

MIDDLETOWN

Middletown, a bucolic spot also on Aquidneck Island, is known for its farms and vineyards, as well as its close proximity to Newport, which is just a few miles down the road. **Sweet Berry Farm** is a family favorite offering pick-your-own berries, seasonal produce, baked goods, and a café. **Newport Vineyard**, a scenic winery with tastings and tours, also has a restaurant featuring farm-to-table cuisine. With miles of hiking trails and educational programs, **Norman Bird Sanctuary**, a 325-acre nature preserve, is a bird-watcher's paradise. Though smaller in scale, the **Paradise Valley Park**, with hiking trails, a freshwater pond, and a picnic area, is also worth a stop. Now that you've worked up an appetite, swing by the iconic **Flo's Clam Shack**, which has been serving delicious fried clams and other seafood dishes for more than eighty years. End the day at **Sachuest Beach** (Second Beach), a beautiful sandy stretch with calm waters.

Flo's Clam Shack

Norman Bird Sanctuary

THE FARM COAST

The **Farm Coast** is a collection of rural communities that runs from Tiverton down to Little Compton in Rhode Island then east into Massachusetts, to include Westport and Dartmouth. The region is named for its bucolic farmland and beachfront living, where historic stone walls and shingled cottages abound. Begin the day at **Tiverton Four Corners**, a historic district that encompasses only a few blocks and features unique boutiques, galleries, and antiques shops. Grab a coffee and pastry at **Groundswell Cafe + Bakery**, a Parisian-inspired eatery that has transformed this corner of Tiverton into both a culinary and creative destination. Stroll through the beautiful gardens to the two other shopfronts: Groundswell Table + Provisions and Groundswell Garden + Home, both of which offer meticulously curated shopping experiences.

From here, hit the open road, explore the scenery, and end the day with sunset at the beach—**Fogland Beach** and **Grinnell's Beach** are both gorgeous. Come spring, roadside farm stands overflow with the area's homegrown produce. Little Compton favorites include

Walker's Roadside, Young Family Farm, Wishing Stone Farm, and Small World Farm. Pull over whenever you see a sign for PYO blueberries, fresh corn, or field-ripened tomatoes. And a bouquet from Little State Flower Company will brighten your day!

As you cross over from Rhode Island into Massachusetts, there are beaches aplenty, from the ever-popular Horseneck Beach to the beach on Gooseberry Island, which is accessible by a causeway connecting the mainland and the island. Spend the day exploring the hundreds of acres of protected beach, fields, woodlands, pond, and marsh at Allens Pond Wildlife Sanctuary. Or weave through the scenic landscape where wineries, such as Running Brook and Westport Rivers, and roadside farm stands abound, as do upscale shops, galleries, and eateries, including Dedee Shattuck Gallery, Davoll's General Store, and Little Moss Restaurant, which is located in Padanaram, a quaint coastal village in South Dartmouth.

Fourth of July Parade

BRISTOL

The town of Bristol, which hosts the oldest Independence Day celebration in the United States, the **Bristol Fourth of July Parade**, is also home to **Blithewold**, a 33-acre oceanfront summer estate featuring a mansion and expansive gardens. The 127-acre historic **Mount Hope Farm** hosts year-round Saturday morning farmers markets. Make a day of it and explore the farm's pathways, trails, and gardens. Stop at **Andrade's Catch**, a family-run fish market in Bristol, which has been around since 1986 and offers the freshest seafood from local waters, supplying retail customers and esteemed restaurants in the Northeast. For boat enthusiasts, the **Herreshoff Marine Museum** is a treasure, dedicated to the history of the

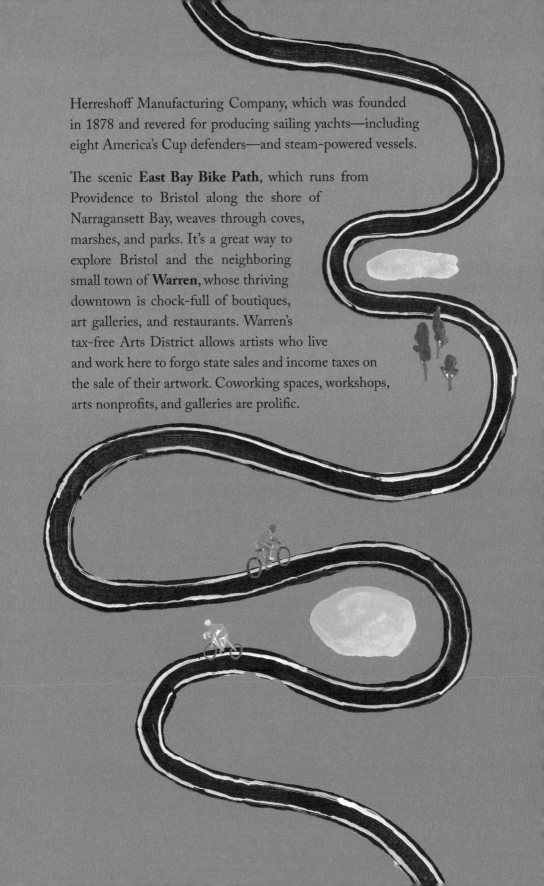

Herreshoff Manufacturing Company, which was founded in 1878 and revered for producing sailing yachts—including eight America's Cup defenders—and steam-powered vessels.

The scenic **East Bay Bike Path**, which runs from Providence to Bristol along the shore of Narragansett Bay, weaves through coves, marshes, and parks. It's a great way to explore Bristol and the neighboring small town of **Warren**, whose thriving downtown is chock-full of boutiques, art galleries, and restaurants. Warren's tax-free Arts District allows artists who live and work here to forgo state sales and income taxes on the sale of their artwork. Coworking spaces, workshops, arts nonprofits, and galleries are prolific.

PROVIDENCE

Just twenty minutes from Bristol, Providence is Rhode Island's capital city, established in 1636 by Roger Williams, a dissident preacher who had to escape Massachusetts because of religious persecution. It was the Narragansett people who helped him survive the cold, harsh winter of his exile. They later allowed Williams to create a settlement on their land, and deeded him the land that became Providence, a new colony with a commitment to liberty in both religious and political realms. History books often paint this as a friendship between the two, but Williams participated in violence against and enslavement of Indigenous people. In downtown Providence, artist Gaia created the *Still Here* **mural**, located on the east wall of 32 Custom House Street. The woman in the painting is Lynsea Montanari of the Narragansett tribe. She's holding a portrait of a Narragansett elder, Princess Red Wing. The mural speaks to the present and future of the land's original inhabitants, the Narragansett. Providence went on to become one of the first industrialized cities in the country, and it was noted for its textile manufacturing and jewelry industry, as well as its working port.

These days, if you scratch the surface of Providence's brusque New England persona, you'll find an intensely creative town, with room for dreamers, artists, culinary enthusiasts, young families, and diverse communities from around the world. The Providence River is the dividing line separating the elegant College Hill (aka the East Side) to its east from downtown, Olneyville, and Federal Hill to its west. Start on College Hill and walk down **Benefit Street**, with its gas lamps and historic homes. **Brown University** and the **Rhode Island School of Design** (RISD) are located on College Hill (hence the name), and their campuses are great for wandering. Brown's **David Winton Bell Gallery** features works by contemporary artists, while just down the street, the **RISD Museum** presents its extensive collection of design objects and fine art alongside contemporary works.

Just a block away, the **Providence Athenaeum**, a historic library that is open to the public, is housed in a stunning Greek Revival building. The surrounding streets are filled with historic and notable homes, such as **Governor Stephen Hopkins House**, the **First Baptist Church in America**, and **Lippitt House Museum**, a Victorian home turned museum, built in 1865.

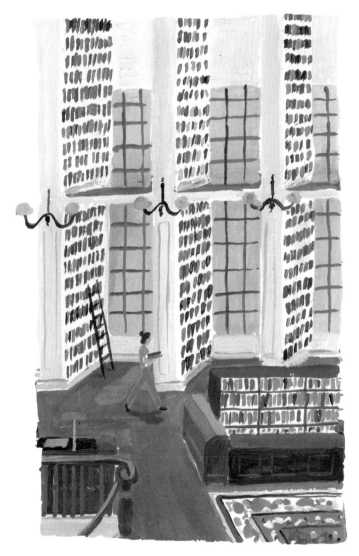

Providence Athenaeum

Roger Williams Park

Providence is a haven for foodies. It's home to **Johnson & Wales**, a culinary university that has schooled many notable chefs, which means the restaurant scene here is always hot. Fine-dining landmark **Al Forno** opened in 1980, and their grilled pizza is legendary. On the flip side of high-end dining, you have **Olneyville New York System**, a local institution that opened in 1946 and is known for its hot wieners—not to be confused with hot dogs—made with a proprietary recipe featuring beef, pork, and veal seasoned with celery salt. You can travel the world through the dining scene, so be sure to explore **Federal Hill** for Italian food, plentiful Portuguese bakeries, and delicious Indian, Bolivian, Oaxacan, Peruvian, and Mexican restaurants along with classic New England seafood joints. You could live here for a decade and not even come close to covering all the incredible dining options, so pace yourself!

Roger Williams Park was created in 1871 and comprises more than 435 acres, an astounding number for a city park. The park today consists of expansive manicured grounds, recreational ponds, public gardens, extensive walkways, tennis courts, ball fields, playgrounds, and public art, as well as historic buildings including the Bandstand, Museum of Natural History and Planetarium, Botanical Center, Temple to Music, and Casino. Don't miss the Roger Williams Park Zoo, home to more than a hundred species from around the world, and the magical indoor **Crescent Park Looff Carousel**, which dates back to 1895.

MASSACHUSETTS

—

the Bay State

Massachusetts

When it comes to blue-blooded, nostalgic Americana, nowhere does it quite like the state that gave us the birthplace of the American Revolution, the Kennedy family, and the movie *Jaws*. An iconic trio! From Boston and Cape Cod to Martha's Vineyard and Salem, there is no shortage of noteworthy stops on your road trip. Indeed, with its unique blend of prominent historical sights and breathtaking natural beauty, Massachusetts, also known as the Bay State, truly captures the essence of New England. Each town has its own unique personality, from the charming streets of Rockport to the vibrant arts scene in Provincetown. You could easily spend months exploring this stretch of coast, as well as its famed islands. Few states offer the same mix of sophisticated, big-city life and quaint, old-fashioned summertime destinations.

Boston often takes center stage, and for good reason. The Freedom Trail, a 2.5-mile path that leads to sixteen significant landmarks including the Massachusetts State House and the Paul Revere House, offers a fascinating glimpse into the role Boston played in the birth of America. Home to world-class museums, such as the Museum of Fine Arts and the Isabella Stewart Gardner Museum, where art collections spanning centuries and cultures are on display, it is a city steeped in history, yet it also boasts a buzzy, cosmopolitan restaurant scene, shopping, and nightlife. It's also a bustling college town, home to Boston University, Tufts, Boston College, and Wellesley, to name just a few institutions. Across the Charles River, Cambridge, a hub of prestigious higher learning, is home to both Harvard and MIT. By population, Massachusetts doesn't even crack the top twenty states; however, Boston has the fourth most colleges and universities of any American city, with 118 located in the greater Boston area at last count.

Beyond Boston, there is plenty to explore as you weave along the coast. Salem, with its witchcraft history, and Plymouth, where the Pilgrims first landed in 1620, are both steeped in American history. Gloucester, a fishing village on Cape Ann, offers dazzling views of the Atlantic Ocean and delicious seafood. And of course no road trip through coastal Massachusetts would be complete without a visit to Cape Cod, a popular summer destination known for its charming towns and the Cape Cod National Seashore, a pristine and protected stretch of coastline that encompasses dunes and wetlands.

Although numerous islands are scattered off the coast of Massachusetts, Martha's Vineyard and Nantucket steal the show. Martha's Vineyard, 20 miles long by 10 miles at its widest point, is twice the size of Nantucket and just 4 miles from the mainland, while Nantucket, the name of which translates from the native Wampanoag language as "faraway place," is 30 miles out to sea.

Gingerbread Cottages at Oak Bluffs,
Martha's Vineyard

Massachusetts

Rhode
Island

Connecticut

Newburyport
the Crane Estate
Cape Ann
Salem
Cambridge
Boston
Duxbury
Plymouth
New Bedford
Dartmouth
Westport
Cape Cod
Martha's Vineyard
Nantucket

Isabella Stewart Gardner Museum

DESTINATIONS

New Bedford
84

Cape Cod
87

Martha's Vineyard
90

Nantucket
94

Plymouth
98

Duxbury
100

Boston
102

Cambridge
108

Salem
110

Cape Ann
113

The Crane Estate
114

Newburyport
115

NEW BEDFORD

Just a couple miles from the Farm Coast town of Westport (see page 68) sits the town of New Bedford. In 1841, this port city was the whaling capital of the world, and it is where author Herman Melville set off on the whaling expedition that would inspire his novel *Moby-Dick*. The **New Bedford Whaling Museum** offers a fascinating look at the history of whaling in the region, as well as current research devoted to the conservation of the area's whale population. The museum is notable for its focus on telling the story from the viewpoints of diverse groups, from abolitionists, environmentalists, and immigrants to fishermen and whalers. New Bedford is also an antiquer's dream, with numerous individual stores as well as warehouses with multi-dealer co-ops, including the 55,000-square-foot **New Bedford Antiques at the Cove**, which houses more than 260 dealers.

New Bedford Whaling Museum

Provincetown

CAPE COD

Accessible by either the Bourne or Sagamore Bridges, and less than an hour from New Bedford (barring bridge traffic), Cape Cod holds a significant place in the collective imagination of New Englanders, having long been considered *the* quintessential summertime destination. It's the land of old-fashioned ice cream shops, whimsical main streets, packed beaches, and lobster rolls served seaside. Driving the length of the Cape is simple and scenic, thanks to Route 6A, also known as Old King's Highway. On the outermost point of the Cape lies the queer enclave of Provincetown, while elsewhere the vibe vacillates between preppy, moneyed, and family-friendly. It's an ecologically fragile peninsula where lively tide pools abound, seals sunbathe on the rocky shores, and migratory shorebirds make their summer homes. The fact that great swathes of the Cape remain untouched by development is due to both its conservation-minded citizens and the legacy of President John F. Kennedy. Having observed the threat to the Cape's fragile ecosystem from his family's summer home in Hyannis Port, Kennedy signed into law a 1961 bill creating the Cape Cod National Seashore, which stretches from Chatham to Provincetown and encompasses around 44,000 acres of coastline, lagoons, salt marshes, forests, and pastures. Included in the preserved area are six coastal towns and ancient burial grounds of Wampanoag and Nauset Indians.

The high season is both glorious (hello, sunshine!) and frustrating, with notorious traffic jams and crowded beaches. Some might argue that the Cape's finest hours occur in the shoulder seasons of April and early May, and again in September and October.

Massachusetts

Sagamore Bridge

Bourne Bridge

Sandwich

Bourne

Mashpee

Falmouth

Woods
Hole

Provincetown

Truro

Wellfleet

Eastham

Cape Cod
National
Seashore

Orleans

Brewster

Cape Cod
Art Center

Dennis

Barnstable

Yarmouth

Atlantic
White Shark
Conservancy

Chatham

Cape Cod

Hyannis Port

Harwich

Kennedy
Compound

MARTHA'S VINEYARD

Celebrities and famous politicians have long made Martha's Vineyard their summer enclave, and the price of oceanside real estate is mind-boggling, but even if you can only afford to visit for the day, it is well worth the ferry ride. And there is an entirely different side to the island, a rugged, close-knit community of year-rounders who give Martha's Vineyard its real charm and character.

Ferries depart from Woods Hole and from North Kingstown, Rhode Island, and dock at Vineyard Haven and Oak Bluffs. Ferry tickets often sell out far in advance during the summer months, so plan ahead. As with so many New England summer hot spots, the shoulder seasons of spring and fall are particularly appealing. If you talk to year-rounders, they will enthusiastically agree. The crowds dissipate; the weather is lovely; and, especially in autumn, the ocean is still warm enough for a dip.

Beyond the beaches, the island has a rich and diverse history. The **Gay Head Cliffs** in Aquinnah are of significant cultural and historical importance, as they are sacred to the Wampanoag tribe, who have lived in the area for thousands of years. You can roam the cliffs, take in the views, and shop at the many stores run by tribal members, such as **Stony Creek Gifts**, where traditional wampum jewelry made from quahog shells is sold.

The **Oak Bluffs** community has long been a summer destination for Black families. Look for plaques around the island marking the thirty-one sites that comprise the **African American Heritage Trail of Martha's Vineyard**, each dedicated to the formerly unrecognized contributions made by Black Americans to the history of the island.

Gay Head Cliffs

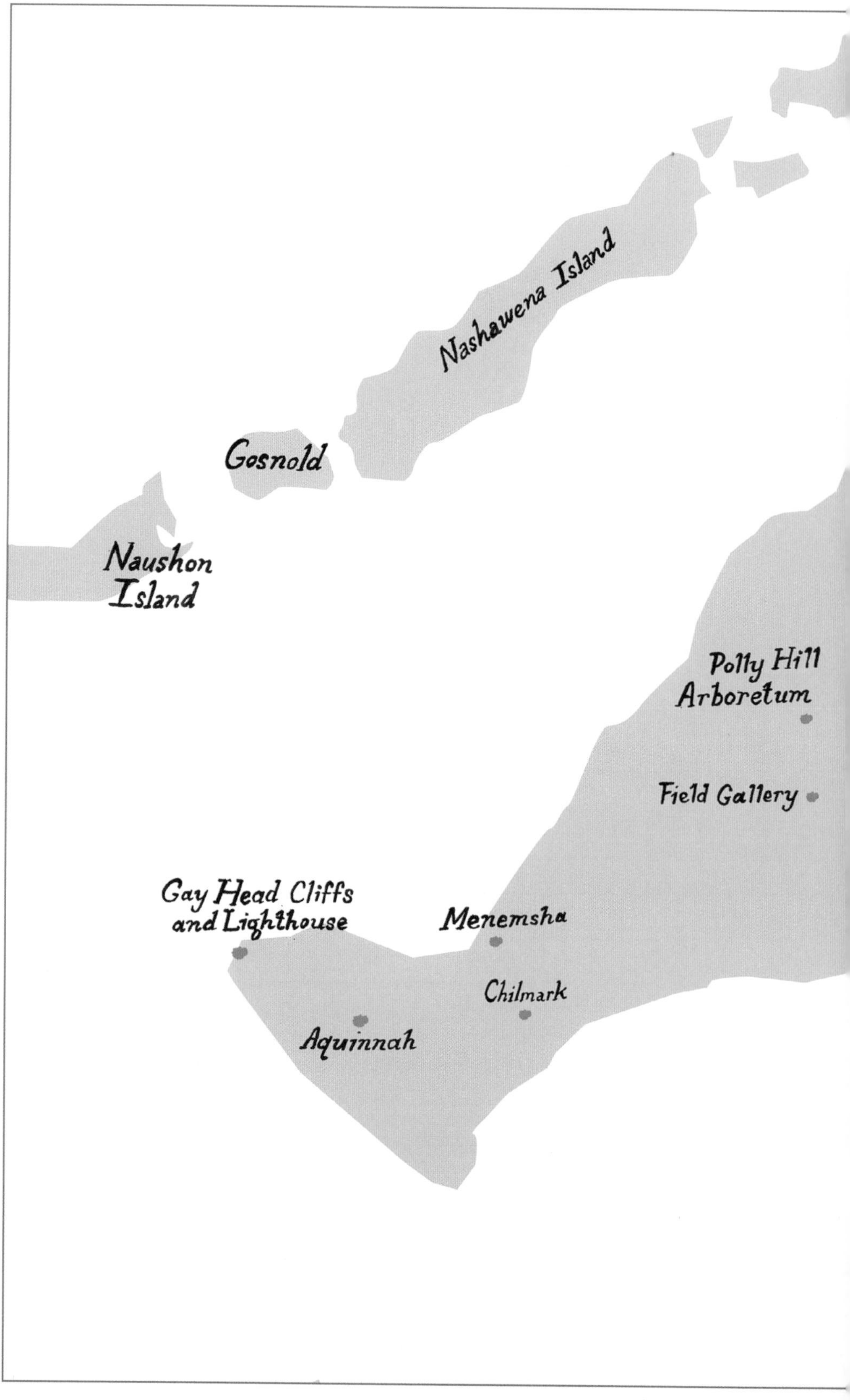

Nashawena Island

Gosnold

Naushon
Island

Polly Hill
Arboretum

Field Gallery

Gay Head Cliffs
and Lighthouse

Menemsha

Chilmark

Aquinnah

Martha's Vineyard

Vineyard
Haven

Bunch of Grapes
Bookstore

Oak Bluffs

Martha's Vineyard
Museum

Jaws Bridge

Edgartown

Chappaquiddick
Island

Edgartown Books

Morning Glory
Farm

Mytoi Japanese
Garden

Sconset

NANTUCKET

Nantucket's cobblestone streets and weathered shingled homes seem to invite a slower pace of life, one that revolves around the island's beaches and natural beauty. That's not to say that Nantucket doesn't rival Martha's Vineyard when it comes to the wealth and fame of its summertime residents, and Nantucket Town is stocked with extravagant shopping, restaurant, and bar options. As with those to Martha's Vineyard, ferries often sell out far in advance during the summer months, so plan ahead. Ferries depart from Hyannis, Harwich Port, and New Bedford. Only locals and summer residents are lucky enough to get their cars onto the island, but it's very easy for visitors get around via bike rentals and a shuttle bus. Everything is accessible by bike. Cycle paths are plentiful, circling and crisscrossing the 3.5-by-14-mile island. Start by renting bikes from **Young's Bicycle Shop**, an island institution that's been around for more than seventy years. From there, take your pick of trails. The **Madaket Road Path**, clocking in at 5.7 miles, is one of the longest and most scenic paths, and ends at **Millie's**, where you can grab a bite and watch the sunset. You'll pass the **Sanford Farm & Ram**

Pasture, a 780-acre Nantucket Conservation Foundation property that boasts a spectacular undeveloped beach at the southern boundary. The **Sconset Path** takes you into Sconset, a village of tiny fishing cottages covered in roses. You can get an ice cream at the **Sconset Market** and a cocktail at the famed **Summer House**.

Once you're in town, park the bike and start walking to sites. (Biking in town can be uncomfortable thanks to the cobblestones.) The **Whaling Museum** documents the island's history as the whaling capital of the world from the mid-1700s to the late 1830s. Vessels would set sail from Nantucket's shores bound for hunting expeditions to the Pacific, returning years later laden with sperm oil. Fans of *Moby-Dick* will want to stop by the **Samuel Owen Gallery**, which is housed in the historic Seven Seas building. Captain George Pollard Jr. of the *Essex*, the sinking of which inspired Melville's saga, once called it home. Nantucket's Main Street—the ten blocks between Quaker Road (Caton Circle) and Straight Wharf—is a defining feature of the island, notable for its looming church spires and historic buildings, many of which are open to visitors. The Nantucket Preservation Trust provides a series of guided and self-guided walking tours that offer a detailed look at the area's historic and architectural heritage. Before you leave, pop by **Murray's Toggery Shop**, the only authentic retailer of the iconic Nantucket Reds, the preppy faded red pants synonymous with the island, and **Mitchell's Book Corner**, beloved by locals and tourists alike for its well-curated sections devoted to Nantucket history and ghost stories. In summertime, local author Elin Hilderbrand does a weekly signing here.

Martha's
Vineyard

Dionis Beach
Jetties Beac
Brant Poin
Mitchell's Book Corn
Madaket Road Path
Sanford
Farm

Ram Pasture

Surfside Bea

Coskata-Coatue
Wildlife Refuge

haling Museum

oung's Bicycle Shop

hildren's Beach

Nantucket Shipwreck
& Lifesaving Museum

Sconset Bluff Walk

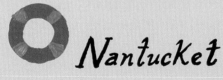

Nantucket

PLYMOUTH

A visit to the historic town of Plymouth is required for anyone interested in early American history. Highlights include **Plymouth Rock**, which is said to have been the landing spot of the Pilgrims in 1620; the **National Monument to the Forefathers**, an 81-foot-tall granite statue built to honor the passengers of the *Mayflower*; and a pair of museums that help illuminate the culture and history of the Wampanoag people.

Pilgrim Hall Museum, the nation's oldest continually operating public museum, opened its doors in 1824. The museum's extraordinary collection of seventeenth-century artifacts, some of which actually were on the *Mayflower*, brings to life the story of early Plymouth Colony and centers on the presence and experiences of the Wampanoag, who called this area home for more than twelve thousand years before the arrival of the English. The Wampanoag Nation once encompassed all of what is now known as southeastern Massachusetts and eastern Rhode Island.

Plimoth Patuxet Museums illuminate the history of Plymouth Colony and the Indigenous Wampanoag people. In the 17th-Century English Village—complete with thatched-roof homes, gardens, and livestock—you can interact with costumed interpreters who demonstrate traditional crafts, cooking, and farming techniques. Step aboard the *Mayflower II*, a full-size reproduction of the ship that brought the Pilgrims to America. Historic Patuxet, a re-creation of a seventeenth-century Native community, features a dome-shaped wetu, the type of house Native people in the Northeast built; a cooking area where you can learn about the Wampanoag seasonal diet; and a demonstration of how a mishoon (dugout canoe) was crafted.

Plimoth Patuxet Museums

DUXBURY

Located on the South Shore of Massachusetts—the stretch of coast between Boston and Cape Cod—is the suburb of Duxbury. This idyllic town is right on Cape Cod Bay, yet it remains unmarred by tourism. Enjoy a beautiful waterfront; the 6-mile-long barrier beach, **Duxbury Beach**; and impossibly fresh seafood. Hit up **Blakeman's** for loaded clam chowder, fresh shucked oysters, and killer lobster rolls—all without the summertime crowds that descend on nearby beach towns. Need to brush up on your sailing, paddleboarding, or kayaking? Head to the **Duxbury Bay Maritime School**, which offers a range of one-day workshops for adults and children, as well as educational programming in subjects such as marine science.

Incorporated in 1637, Duxbury was one of the first towns settled once the Pilgrims began to disperse from neighboring Plymouth. History runs deep here, and several of the town's oldest houses—the **King Caesar**, **Bradford**, and **Nathaniel Winsor Jr. Houses**—have been preserved and turned into museums. Having recently undergone a major renovation, the **Art Complex Museum** features an extensive collection of American art and Shaker furniture.

SEA LIFE
in tide pools

Bladderwrack

Sea anemones

Mummichogs

Periwinkles

Dog whelks

Jonah crabs

Starfish

BOSTON

From Duxbury, it is a short drive into Boston, inevitable traffic notwithstanding. While the city needs no introduction, it's important to understand its immense historical and cultural significance before diving into its greatest sites.

Boston has a rich and complex history that spans nearly four centuries, and its identity is as unique and multifaceted as the people who call it home. Throughout its long existence, Boston has undergone numerous transformations, from serving as the cradle of the American Revolution to being recognized as an international center of higher learning and an exciting gastronomic destination. From the bustling wharves that once bore witness to famous tea parties to the Federal-style brick row houses of Beacon Hill, Boston is one of the country's most enduring cities.

Each year, Boston's famed universities attract an astounding 150,000 students from the world over, infusing the city with a youthful vigor and international feel. It is a town that is passionate about its sports,

Beacon Hill

from baseball (as played by the Boston Red Sox, breakers of professional sports' most infamous curse) to the annual Boston Marathon, which is traditionally held on Patriots' Day, the third Monday of April. If you visit during baseball season, be sure to catch a game at the iconic **Fenway Park**. It's madness on game days, and Boston fans are a wild bunch, but it is always a blast.

Begin your visit by walking the 2.5-mile **Freedom Trail** to orient yourself to the city's illustrious history and the role it played in the birth of America, and poke around the shops at **Faneuil Hall Marketplace**, next to the Faneuil Hall stop on the trail. You can hardly turn a corner without running into a world-class museum. You could easily spend a week just bopping from one to another, and here's a hot tip: The CityPASS makes museum-hopping easy and more affordable.

A stroll through the **Public Garden** is the prettiest way to get from one side of town to the other; you'll pass a lagoon, which is where the famous Swan Boats are located. Stop into the hallowed halls of the **Boston Public Library**, the oldest municipally funded lending library in the country. The main-branch **McKim Building** is an

McKim Building

iconic masterpiece of Gilded Age architect Charles Follen McKim. Nearby **Beacon Hill** is a treasure trove of high-end shops and charming restaurants, including the impeccably designed **Beacon Hill Books & Cafe**. Newbury Street offers more highbrow shops, with a few indie gems among them, like the awesome **Newbury Comics**.

In Boston's "Little Italy," the **North End**, you'll find old-school Italian restaurants and pizzerias packed along narrow streets. Stop in the **Old North Church**, whose gift shop is surprisingly listed as one of the best shops in all of Boston! Tucked in between Back Bay, Chinatown, South Boston, and Roxbury (Mission Hill, which is part of Roxbury, is where disco legend Donna Summer grew up)—all worth a stop, I might add—is the **South End**, a landmarked historic district with the country's largest collection of Victorian-era row houses.

Not far from West Roxbury is the **Arnold Arboretum of Harvard University**, a gorgeous 281-acre green space with a number of walking and biking trails, and the oldest public arboretum in North America (established in 1872). It is the crown jewel of renowned landscape architect Frederick Law Olmsted's famed **Emerald Necklace**, which encompasses 1,100 acres of parkland extending from the Boston Common through the Back Bay Fens and Jamaica Pond Park to Franklin Park in Dorchester.

The **Charles River Esplanade**, located along the Boston side of the Charles River Basin between the Museum of Science and the Boston University Bridge, is a vibrant green space that contains the Hatch Shell, which hosts summer concerts, while a jogging path runs riverside along the park's length. Dotted with sculptures, benches, and playgrounds, it affords a beautiful view of Cambridge. A walk along the river is a lovely way to end a busy day of sightseeing.

Boston Museums

Exploring Boston's diverse array of museums provides a captivating journey through art, science, and history, offering enriching experiences that appeal to a wide range of interests.

Institute of Contemporary Art

Housed in a strikingly modern building in South Boston's Seaport District, the museum is dedicated to providing public access to leading contemporary artists and emerging voices.

Museum of Fine Arts Boston

Containing nearly 500,000 works of art, the museum's renowned collection spans from ancient artistry to modern masterpieces.

Isabella Stewart Gardner Museum

Founded by Gardner, a notable art collector and philanthropist, this museum is home to one of the world's most remarkable art collections.

Boston Children's Museum

Packed with hands-on exhibits and programs that encourage young children to learn about science, exploration, nature, and more, through play.

Museum of Science

With a mission to inspire a lifelong love of science, this museum contains more than 700 interactive exhibits, plus daily presentations and an IMAX theater.

CAMBRIDGE

Start the morning with a walk over the **John W. Weeks Memorial Bridge**, usually referred to as the Weeks Bridge, which spans the Charles River. Located on the stunning campus of prestigious **Harvard University**, it is always filled with joggers and pedestrians eager to catch the sun's first rays. While on campus, pay a visit to the iconic **Harvard Yard**, as well as the **Harvard Museum of Natural History**, the **Harvard Art Museums**, and the **Peabody Museum**, which contains an incredible collection of anthropological materials from across the world. **Harvard Square** is where all the college kids congregate, which means it is full of coffee shops, independent bookstores, and fast-casual dining spots. Head over to the nearby **MIT Museum**, which aims to showcase that university's legacy and accomplishments. The museum features exhibits on cutting-edge technology, technology-related artworks, artificial intelligence, architecture, and robotics, as well as fascinating artifacts from the history of science and engineering.

One of the most notable historic sites in Cambridge is the **Longfellow House–Washington's Headquarters National Historic Site**. Built in 1759, the house was used as the headquarters of George Washington during the Revolutionary War from July 1775 to April 1776 and was the home of poet Henry Wadsworth Longfellow for four decades in the 1800s.

Central Square, located at the intersection of Massachusetts Avenue, Prospect Street, and Western Avenue, often gets overshadowed by the more famous Harvard Square. However, it is a vibrant and diverse neighborhood, with a wide variety of bars, restaurants, live music, theater venues, and shops, as well as an eclectic nightlife scene. You can easily spend an afternoon just wandering the square, stopping for coffee and lunch, and popping into cool independently owned shops.

Harvard Yard

Salem is roughly 20 miles north of Boston, but time your drive to avoid Boston's notoriously horrendous rush hour traffic. Hit the MA 1A at the wrong time, and those 20 miles could take you well over an hour.

Massachusetts is rife with personality-filled towns, none so much as spooky, haunted Salem, site of the infamous witch trials of 1692, during which more than two hundred people were accused of practicing witchcraft. A walk along the **Salem Heritage Trail**—just follow the bright red line—will take you by all the major landmarks. The **Jonathan Corwin House**, aka the Witch House, is Salem's only remaining building with direct ties to the trials. Judge Corwin was called on to investigate the alleged witchcraft and served on the court that sentenced nineteen people to the gallows. The **Salem Witch Museum**, which opened in 1972, brings to life the events leading up to and following the trials. It is often packed, so make sure to secure your tickets in advance. The **House of the Seven Gables** (aka the Turner-Ingersoll Mansion) is a beautifully restored 1668 home made famous by Nathaniel Hawthorne's 1851 novel of the same name. The home and its verdant seaside gardens are open for tours.

In an incredible feat of preservation, Salem boasts four local historic districts—**Derby Street**, **Lafayette Street**, **McIntire**, and **Washington Square**—which comprise more than six hundred historic and architecturally significant buildings, as well as beautiful parks and cemeteries.

The **Peabody Essex Museum**, which grew out of the East India Marine Society, a group of eighteenth-century Salem sea captains who collected curiosities during their sailing expeditions, houses a substantial collection of global art and artifacts, including a rebuilt Qing dynasty–era Chinese house. The **McIntire Historic District** is located just a short walk from the Peabody Essex's main campus, and showcases Georgian- and Federal-period houses designed or influenced by renowned architect Samuel McIntire, as well as the lovely Ropes Garden.

Woodman's
of Essex

Wingaersheek
Beach

Plum Cove
Beach

Rockport · Shalin Liu
Performance Center

Man at the
Wheel statue

Good Harbor
Beach

Rocky Neck
Art Colony

Gloucester
Harbor

Stage Fort Park

Singing Beach

CAPE ANN

While you're welcome to battle the summertime traffic on Cape Cod, there is an alternative cape that offers beautiful beaches and fried clams aplenty. Even for most New Englanders, Cape Ann flies a bit under the radar—though among those who know it, the love for this rocky peninsula runs deep. Rockport clings to the eastern-most part of Cape Ann. Neighboring Gloucester, New England's most famous fishing village, occupies the rest of what amounts to a large island. Across the Annisquam River, the town of Essex is known for its antiques and famous **Woodman's** fried clams, while Manchester-by-the-Sea embraces its seafaring nomenclature.

Rockport's scenic main harbor, home to the iconic brick-red fish shack known as **Motif Number 1**—a replica of a former 1840 fishing shack that was known as "the most often-painted building in America"—is connected to **Bearskin Neck**, a stretch of boutique shops and cozy restaurants.

Situated on a peninsula within Gloucester's working harbor, the colorful, eclectic **Rocky Neck Art Colony** is one of the oldest continually operating art colonies in the country, once home to notable plein air artists including Winslow Homer and Edward Hopper. Fitz Henry Lane, whose house stands on a hill above the harbor, is considered to be among the greatest of all maritime painters. Many of his works are on display at the **Cape Ann Museum** on Gloucester's Pleasant Street. **Stage Fort Park** provides sweeping views of Gloucester Harbor and the *Man at the Wheel* **statue**, aka the Gloucester Fishermen's Memorial, which honors those lost at sea from 1623 to 1923. Six of the plaques, dated 1991, honor the captain and crew of the Gloucester-based *Andrea Gail*, the fishing boat made famous in the book and film *The Perfect Storm*. In 2001, a memorial honoring the fishermen's wives was erected near the statue.

THE CRANE ESTATE

Just over a dozen miles from Cape Ann, this awe-inspiring 2,100-acre seaside estate includes **Crane Beach**, where you'll find trails and boardwalks that weave through a landscape of sand dunes; **Castle Hill**, once the lavish summer home for Chicago industrialist Richard Teller Crane Jr., with manicured gardens and a generous lawn sloping down to the seashore; the **Crane Wildlife Refuge**, a protected landscape of salt marsh and coastal islands including Choate Island and Long Island; and the **Inn at Castle Hill**, an elegant lodging option.

NEWBURYPORT

Newburyport is home to a lovely downtown and waterfront, but the real draw of the area is the coastal landscape and beaches. Located just a few miles from downtown Newburyport, **Plum Island,** named for the beach plum shrubs that grow in the dunes, is a barrier island that is home to sandy beaches, wildlife refuges, and nature reserves. Catch sunset at the **Plum Island Lighthouse,** built in 1898 and also known as the Newburyport Harbor Lighthouse. It is located across from the **Parker River National Wildlife Refuge**—teeming with more than three hundred species of birds, including the threatened piping plover shorebird—at the northern section of Plum Island. On the southern tip of the island, the 77-acre **Sandy Point State Reservation** has a beautiful beach.

The Dune Shacks
OF PEAKED HILL BARS HISTORIC DISTRICT

These historic dune shacks once housed famed writers and artists—including Henry David Thoreau, Tennessee Williams, Eugene O'Neill, Jack Kerouac, Mary Oliver, Norman Mailer, and Jackson Pollock—during Provincetown's artistic heyday. Nestled between Provincetown and Truro in the protected Cape Cod National Seashore, these shacks were originally built in the late 1800s as lifesaving huts for shipwreck survivors. The nineteen shacks that remain today (all but one owned by the National Park Service) were constructed beginning in the 1920s, supposedly using the scraps of shipwrecks that washed up on the beach. The shacks are primitive, with no electricity or plumbing, and isolated, allowing for spartan solitude and communion with nature. Community residencies are open to all and are filled through a lottery system, while artists, writers, and poets can apply through designated residencies. The only way to reach the shacks is by hiking a few miles over the dunes or by a trip with Art's Dune Tours.

Fowler Dune Shack

Euphoria

Leo Fleurant Shack

David and Marcia Adams
guest cottage

C-Scape Dune Shack

NEW HAMPSHIRE

—

the Granite State

WELCOME TO

New Hampshire

New Hampshire, the Granite State, is a paradise for those who enjoy outdoor adventures. The White Mountains house the highest peak in New England—the majestic Mount Washington—as well as some of the most scenic landscapes in the Northeast, including Franconia Notch State Park, the Kancamagus Highway, and the Flume Gorge. Each season brings its own unique beauty and recreational opportunities. During the summer months, the Lakes Region, which includes Lake Winnipesaukee, Lake Winnisquam, Squam Lake, and Newfound Lake, among many smaller lakes, is a popular vacation spot for water-sports enthusiasts and those who want to explore its quaint towns. In fall, take a scenic drive, hike, or bike ride through the mountains to fully experience the state's stunning foliage, with forests ablaze in vibrant reds, oranges, and yellows. For skiers and snowboarders, the winter months bring some of the best snow in the Northeast, with popular resorts such as Bretton Woods, Loon Mountain, and Cannon Mountain offering a plethora of options for hitting the slopes.

It's a shame that many of the state's true gems are located beyond the coastline, which is only around 15 miles long, stretching from Seabrook to historic Portsmouth. If you have the time, venture inland and enjoy all that New Hampshire has to offer. If not, the coast will give you just enough of a taste of the "Live Free or Die" state to leave you wanting more.

Great North Woods

White Mountains

Kancamaqus

New Hampshire

Connecticut
River

North Hampton

Maine

lsmouth

DESTINATIONS

North Hampton
126

Rye
127

Portsmouth
128

Keep Going . . .
FAVORITE INLAND SPOTS
IN NEW HAMPSHIRE
132

Sea Shell Stage

NORTH HAMPTON

From Newburyport, Massachusetts, take NH 1A about 9 miles until you reach **Hampton Beach State Park** and the **Sea Shell Stage**, where concerts are held every night of the week from late May through early September. From classic rock to country, doo-wop to reggae, the musical range is vast, and a good time is guaranteed.

Head just a few miles north along the coast and you'll come to **Fuller Gardens**, a public coastal botanical garden dating back to 1927. Once part of the summer estate of Alvan T. Fuller, the grounds were designed by noted landscape designers Arthur Shurtleff and the Olmsted brothers. While the estate, known as Runnymede-by-the-Sea, has been leveled, the Carriage House (circa 1890) still stands, as does the Union Chapel. Open from mid-May through mid-October, the sprawling gardens include seventeen hundred rosebushes, a dahlia display, formal English perennial borders, a Japanese garden, and a tropical conservatory, all of which are framed by sculpted hedges that abut the sea.

RYE

Follow the coastline just a few miles north to Rye, home to **Jenness State Beach** and **Wallis Sands State Beach**, as well as **Odiorne Point State Park**, a recreational area with 135 acres of trails along the rocky shoreline. The **Seacoast Science Center**, which is located within the park, has exhibits featuring fish and marine mammals, plus saltwater touch tanks. Conservation and education are at the heart of the science center's mission, as seen through interactive exhibits on reef restoration, the impact of climate change on the Gulf of Maine, and the efforts directed at protecting humpback whales and other marine mammals.

PORTSMOUTH

Continue north just a few miles on NH 1A to Portsmouth. Settled in 1623, Portsmouth was originally a working seaport, and still today you can watch from the harbor as tugboats escort ships along the deepwater Piscataqua River. The settlement's initial name, Strawbery Banke, was inspired by the abundance of wild strawberries that grew along the waterfront. The name was changed to Portsmouth in 1653, in honor of the colony's founder, John Mason, who was the captain of the English port of Portsmouth, Hampshire. Visit the **Strawbery Banke Museum**, an outdoor living-history museum spread over 10 acres, and peruse the dozens of historic buildings, gardens, and exhibits that illustrate life in Portsmouth from the seventeenth to the twenty-first century. Tour the **Wentworth-Coolidge Mansion**, an eighteenth-century harborfront estate that is open for guided tours and offers a scenic waterfront trail. For a greater glimpse into the city's colonial past, the **Portsmouth Harbour Trail** encompasses more than seventy points of historical significance. From June through October, tours depart from the Market Square information kiosk.

Take a stroll through **Market Square** to discover unique shops, art galleries, and restaurants. Keep an eye out for the many well-preserved eighteenth- and nineteenth-century buildings, which add to the architectural appeal of the city, such as the old Custom House and Post Office. End the day on the waterfront at **Prescott Park**, which offers beautiful gardens, walking paths, and a performance space that hosts outdoor concerts and plays in the summer months.

Strawbery Banke Museum

The **Isles of Shoals**, a group of nine rocky isles located 6 miles off the New Hampshire and Maine coasts, can be glimpsed from Portsmouth. Over the years, they have served as a base for fishermen, a haven for pirates, a summer retreat for artists and the wealthy, and, for more than a century, the site of a Unitarian conference center. Unfortunately, the privately owned islands are not accessible to the public, and there is no year-round population on the Shoals, apart from a rich variety of shorebirds, marine invertebrates, and hundreds of harbor and gray seals.

Maine's Appledore Island is home to the **Shoals Marine Laboratory**, where students and scientists study the diverse ecosystem. The Shoals hold a significant place in the seacoast community's lore, due in part to the double murder that occurred on Smuttynose Island in the 1800s and the isles' rich literary history. Celia Thaxter, New Hampshire's most famous writer and poet of the nineteenth century and daughter of lighthouse keeper Thomas Laighton, was raised on White Island. When her father resigned as keeper, he built a large hotel on Appledore Island, which became a gathering place for the literary and artistic greats of New England, such as Nathaniel Hawthorne, Harriet Beecher Stowe, Henry David Thoreau, and Childe Hassam. The garden that inspired Thaxter's best-known book, *An Island Garden*, still exists today on Appledore Island, and looks much as it did more than a century ago.

Isles of Shoals

FAVORITE INLAND SPOTS IN NEW HAMPSHIRE

One of the best ways to experience New Hampshire's interior charm is to follow one of its many scenic routes that showcase its natural beauty through majestic mountains, pristine lakes, and sweeping forests. Journey along the winding roads that lead through the White Mountains, or weave through the lakes region, following the shores of Lake Winnisquam, Ossipee Lake, Squam Lake, and more. As you traverse the state, you'll encounter quaint covered bridges, historic mills, and cozy inns that exude New England charm. From the serene shores of Lake Winnipesaukee to the rugged beauty of Franconia Notch State Park, here are a few places to visit as you road-trip through New Hampshire.

Connecticut River Byway

This stunning route follows the Connecticut River, which weaves through Connecticut, Massachusetts, and Vermont as well as New Hampshire, and is dotted with hiking trails, scenic vistas, fly-fishing spots, and covered bridges, including the Cornish-Windsor, one of the longest in the country. Explore the quaint New Hampshire towns that dot the route, such as Haverhill, with its historic Main Street lined with shops and eateries, and Hanover, home to Dartmouth College and its picturesque campus. Along the way, stop at various state parks and nature reserves, such as Saint-Gaudens National Historical Park, where you can enjoy hiking, wildlife spotting, or picnicking by the riverside.

Great North Woods Ride

This scenic 120-mile loop takes you north of the White Mountain National Forest to the Great North Woods. As you venture along this route, keep your eyes peeled for native wildlife, such as black bears, deer, and moose, which are commonly spotted in the area. Don't miss the renowned "Moose Alley," a stretch of the drive known for frequent moose sightings. Along the route, you'll pass through Gorham, Errol, Colebrook, and the historically significant mill city of Berlin, known as the City That Trees Built.

Kancamagus Scenic Byway

One of the best road trips in New Hampshire, and a perennial favorite with leaf peepers, this 34.5-mile stretch follows New Hampshire's Route 112 and passes through the heart of the White Mountains between the towns of Lincoln and Conway. Fall foliage explodes with color as the winding road varies in elevation, though the scenery is also beautiful in winter, when snow covers the ground and caps the mountains. There are ample opportunities for hiking and pulling off the road for photographs, like at Pemigewasset Overlook, a great spot for watching the sun set. Attractions along the route include the Albany Covered Bridge, Sabbaday Falls, Rocky Gorge, Swift River, and Mount Kancamagus.

White Mountains Trail

This 100-mile drive crosses through three notable mountain passes—or notches—and skirts the Appalachian Trail. You'll encounter popular attractions like the Mount Washington Cog Railway, where you can ascend Mount Washington, the highest peak in the Northeast. Visit the Mount Washington Observatory at the summit. Take in the awe-inspiring views from spots like Franconia Notch State Park, known for its dramatic mountain passes and the iconic (now collapsed) Old Man of the Mountain.

Lakes Loop

New Hampshire is home to many of New England's most stunning lakes. This 134-mile route takes you through the lakes region dotted with some of the most notable bodies of water, including Lake Winnipesaukee, Squam Lake, Lake Winnisquam, Ossipee Lake, and Newfound Lake. On the shores of Lake Winnipesaukee, wind around to Wolfeboro, the oldest summer resort town in America, attracting summering crowds since the 1700s. Near Moultonborough, take a detour to visit the Castle in the Clouds mansion and museum. Climb the nearby East Rattlesnake Trail in Holderness for sweeping views. Stop in Gilford and enjoy the expansive sandy beach at Ellacoya State Park. And explore charming lakeside towns such as Meredith and Center Harbor. Pack a swimsuit and take the opportunity to engage in water activities like boating, fishing, and swimming in the crystal-clear water.

MAINE

—

the Pine Tree State

Maine

Maine summers are a treat for the senses: a weathered cottage on a rocky shore, hot butter drizzled over sweet lobster meat, tiny wild blueberries picked by the bucketful, the salty brine of cool ocean air, sunshine toasting the tip of your nose, and the enveloping aroma of evergreens. (Maine's official nicknames are the Pine Tree State and Vacationland for good reason.) What sets this state apart? It's the coastline of working harbors, rocky shores, and thousands of micro-islands, plus scenic villages, legendary artists' colonies, and unspoiled wilderness. With 3,500 miles of tidal land, more than sixty lighthouses, and 90 percent of the country's blueberries and lobsters, Maine is an iconic summertime destination. Even in the warmest months, the water here is bracingly chilly, which is perhaps the reason Mainers have earned themselves a rugged reputation. That, and the intense winters. Exploring all the region has to offer could take an entire summer, though the other three seasons have their own appeal, too.

Beginning in York, the journey northward will take you through four distinct regions: the Maine Beaches, the only bit of coast with sandy beaches; Greater Portland—a diverse and vibrant city known for its food scene—and Casco Bay; Mid-coast Maine, a place of hardworking fishing villages and rocky shorelines; and Down East and Acadia, a vast, stunning, protected landscape of granite coastal cliffs, islands, estuary and intertidal habitats, and the tallest peak on the Atlantic coast of the United States, Cadillac Mountain.

Acadia National Park lies in the Wabanaki homeland, and the park offers several fascinating programs that allow visitors to learn from Wabanaki ecologists and archaeologists. Indigenous peoples made their home for thousands of years in what is now called Maine. The Abenaki, Maliseet, Mi'kmaq, Passamaquoddy, and Penobscot Nations are collectively called the Wabanaki, "People of the Dawnland." The tribes relied on the area's rich natural resources for hunting, fishing, gathering berries, and harvesting clams and other shellfish. When European colonizers started arriving in the 1600s, the Wabanaki survived multiple attempts to displace and erase them. Begin your visit to Acadia by spending time at the Abbe Museum, which has two locations, one in downtown Bar Harbor and one in Acadia National Park, dedicated to showcasing the history and cultures of the Wabanaki.

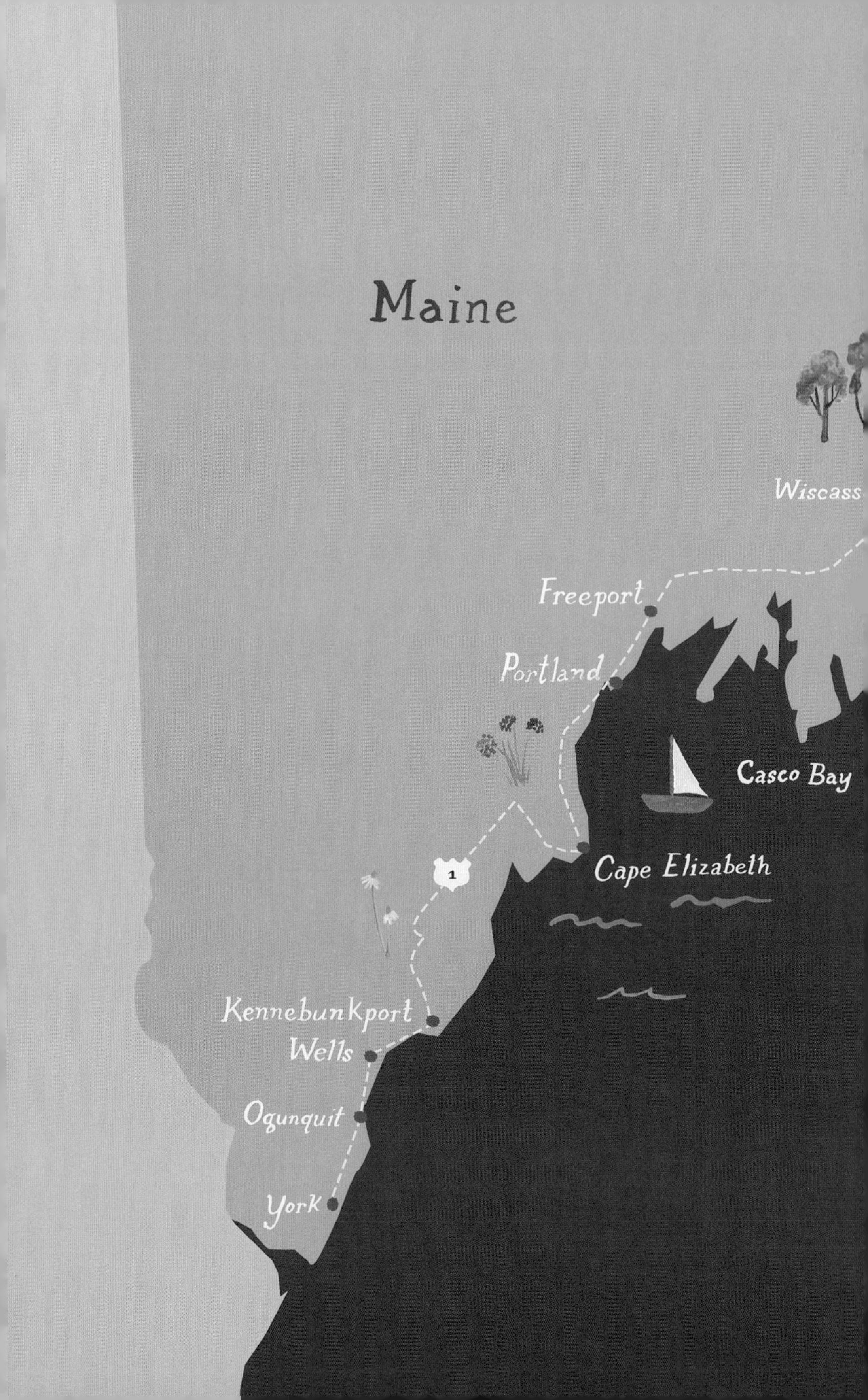

Maine

Wiscass

Freeport

Portland

Casco Bay

Cape Elizabeth

1

Kennebunkport
Wells

Ogunquit

York

Unity

The Common
Ground Fair

Belfast

Bar
Harbor

Acadia
National
Park

Waldoboro

Rockland

othbay Harbor

DESTINATIONS

York
146

Ogunquit
148

Wells
151

Kennebunkport
152

Portland
154

Freeport
158

Wiscasset
159

Boothbay Harbor
160

Rockland
162

Belfast
163

Bar Harbor
166

YORK

Nothing says summer in New England quite like the chewy, sweet pull of saltwater taffy. You can't pass through York without stopping in at longtime favorite the **Goldenrod**, a candy store and café that has been open since 1896. Annually, they produce about 8 million pieces of their famous saltwater taffy, which is made on-site. For more classic summertime fun, visit **Short Sands Beach**, home to **Fun-O-Rama**, an old-school arcade right on the sand. Both Short Sands Beach and Long Sands Beach offer views of the **Nubble Light**, which sits on its own tiny island off Cape Neddick. Surf culture gets a handcrafted touch at **Grain Surfboards**, where they make boards from local wood. And the flagship store of **Stonewall Kitchen**, the iconic specialty food producer known for its jams and jellies, is right in town and has a café, cooking classes, and a showroom. With more than 40 miles of trails, the 10,000-acre **Mount Agamenticus** is a landscape of coastal forest that supports the state's largest diversity of animal and plant species.

Grain Surfboards

Maine Foods

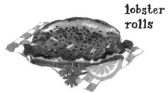

lobster rolls

wild "lowbush" blueberries

Tiny and sweet, these precious fruits grow in the peaty soil that forms Maine's vast blueberry barrens. Savor them in pies and pancakes, preserve them for winter, or eat them fresh by the bushel.

The quintessential summer treat is a buttery, grilled split-top bun piled high with lobster meat. Be sure to eat it seaside, because every great roll deserves a great view.

chowder

Though it's popular across New England, nowhere does chowder quite like Maine, thanks to its abundance of fresh seafood. Consisting of a creamy, briny base packed with potato and fish, plus chewy gems of clam, corn, and pork, this peppery, salty delicacy is best topped with a handful of oyster crackers.

oysters

Maine oysters—Damariscotta being the most popular variety—are known for their plump, sweet meat, bright briny flavor, and strong shells. With more than 150 oyster farms throughout the state, Maine raises more than 11 million oysters per year.

potato doughnuts

whoopie pies

While doughnuts made with mashed potatoes or potato flour are nothing new, Portland-based the Holy Donut made these a statewide obsession. Founder Leigh Kellis's unique recipe relies on riced potatoes.

Designated in 2011 as Maine's official state treat, this sweet confection consists of white cream filling thickly sandwiched between two chocolate cake–like rounds.

OGUNQUIT

A mere 7 miles up the coast from York is the tiny town of Ogunquit. In the Abenaki language, the word *Ogunquit* translates to "beautiful place by the sea," so it should come as no surprise that it's home to one of the most gorgeous beaches in the country. **Ogunquit Beach**, a 3.5-mile-long stretch of pristine soft, sandy coastline, is unusual for Maine, since typically the coastline here is very rocky. **Footbridge Beach** also boasts soft, sandy shores. In contrast, the 1.25-mile paved pedestrian path, the **Marginal Way**, follows the rocky outcrop and provides access to dramatic scenic overlooks. The path connects Ogunquit town center with **Perkins Cove**, a small turn-of-the-century fishing village with its own charming shops, restaurants, and wooden double-leaf pedestrian drawbridge that spans the narrow entrance to the port.

Ogunquit originated as a shipbuilding colony in 1641, and later flourished as an artistic community. The **Ogunquit Museum of American Art** showcases works by homegrown artists dating back as far as the 1800s. It has a rotation of seasonal exhibits and permanent collections, as well as a 3-acre sculpture park that includes numerous gardens. Ditch the car and take a ride on the **Ogunquit Trolley**, which hits all the popular spots, like Ogunquit Beach, the Marginal Way, and Perkins Cove, and runs in summer from 9 a.m. to 8 p.m. most days.

Ogunquit Museum of American Art

Perkins Cove

bald eagle

monarch butterfly

gray
fox

Indiana
bat

Atlantic salmon

black
bear

WELLS

From Ogunquit, take a short 5-mile drive north along Route 1 to Wells. While there are beautiful beaches here—Wells Beach, Drakes Island Beach, Moody Beach, and the rather rocky Crescent Beach, to name a few—the real draw of this friendly small town known as the Antiques Capital of Maine is its abundance of antiques shops. You'll find more than twenty-five along Route 1 as you head into and out of town. On the way into Kennebunkport, your next stop, plan to spend an afternoon at the **Rachel Carson National Wildlife Refuge** that encompasses more than 9,000 acres of salt marshes, barrier beaches, tidal estuaries, and dunes offering protected habitat to an astounding number of migratory birds including sandpipers, terns, shearwaters, and ospreys, as well as puffins, owls, falcons, and egrets. This is a birder's and hiker's paradise.

KENNEBUNKPORT

Walker's Point Estate, otherwise known as the Bush family compound, thrust the coastal town of Kennebunkport into the national spotlight when George H. W. Bush became president in 1989. A drive east down **Ocean Avenue** will take you right past the Bushes' summer retreat and allow you to peek at the other beautiful homes with magnificent water views. Back in town, stroll through the boutiques, art galleries, and knickknack shops in **Dock Square**, a walkable retail area near Kennebunk's Lower Village and Kennebunkport's downtown neighborhoods.

Beautiful beaches are plentiful here, favorites being **Kennebunk Beach**; **Colony Beach**, ideally located for catching beautiful sunsets; **Goose Rocks Beach**; and the peaceful, tucked-away **Parsons Beach**.

On the way out of town, stop at **Cape Porpoise**, a tiny working fishing village where you can see Kennebunkport's fishermen hauling in lobster traps and tuning up their boats. As you can imagine, the seafood fare here is supremely fresh, served simply and without a lot of fuss. Head out to the tip of the pier for a nice view of the **Goat Island Lighthouse**.

PORTLAND

Easily one of America's best food cities, Portland boasts a plethora of incredible restaurants, coffee shops, bakeries, microbreweries, and seafood stands. Finding a great meal here is as easy as shooting fish in a barrel. And I'm not just talking about lobster rolls, although the working harbor's crews still haul in boatloads of Maine's sweet, juicy lobster. Once known as Machigonne (Great Neck) by its Indigenous inhabitants, the Algonquians, the peninsula was claimed in 1632 by the British, who founded a settlement on Casco Bay. It thrived, transforming the once sleepy waterfront into a hub for fishing and trading companies. The food scene here doesn't ascribe to trends, instead focusing on the region's rich agricultural offerings and plentiful seafood. Walk around the cobblestone streets of the **Old Port**, pop into the ever-changing group of eateries and breweries, and be sure to leave room for a potato doughnut from the famed **Holy Donut**. With breweries aplenty, you can't beat the OG of Portland's craft beer movement, **Allagash Brewing Company**.

Portland is a deeply creative town, and a wander through the **Arts District** will illuminate the depth of its creativity. And don't miss the city's thriving independent bookstore scene, which includes Print: A Bookstore, Longfellow Books, Sherman's of Portland, Back Cove Books, and Letterpress Books. Visit the oldest public art institution in the United States, the **Portland Museum of Art**, founded in 1882 and home to an impressive collection that includes works by Andy Warhol, N. C. Wyeth, Winslow Homer, and Claude Monet.

Set sail on one of **Portland Schooner Co.**'s handcrafted wooden crafts built right here in Maine; *Timberwind* and *Wendameen* are listed on the National Register of Historic Places. The two-hour Windjammer cruise on Casco Bay is the perfect way to experience the beauty of Portland's rugged coastline.

The **Portland Freedom Trail** is a deeply moving self-guided tour that pays tribute to Black Mainers who fought to end slavery in the nineteenth century. The thirteen locations along the trail honor the state's abolitionist history and highlight Maine's role in the

Portland Schooner

Underground Railroad, in which formerly enslaved individuals traveled along several hidden routes that stretched north across the border to Canada.

For a truly unique Vacationland experience, hop on the **Casco Bay Lines Mailboat Run,** a working ferry that leaves from Portland and delivers mail and freight to the islands of Little Diamond, Great Diamond, Long, Cliff, and Chebeague. It's a splendid way to experience Casco Bay. You can also catch a ferry over to Peaks Island, which makes a lovely day trip. The best way to experience the island is a golf cart tour. And don't leave without indulging in one of the famous cinnamon buns from the always-packed **Peaks Cafe**. But get there early—most days the buns sell out in a hot minute!

Maine's Best Farmers Markets

Beyond Portland—whose farmers market dates back to 1768—smaller coastal towns also offer an abundance of Maine-grown produce and products at lovely farmers markets, which speaks to the region's deep and rich agricultural roots.

Belfast

Portland

Rockland

Camden

FREEPORT

Roughly 15 miles from Portland, you'll know you've arrived in Freeport when the giant duck boot comes into view. That is, the marker of beloved outdoor company **L.L. Bean**'s flagship store, which is far from Freeport's only lure but certainly its most well known. L.L. Bean anchors the shopping at **Freeport Village Station**. Put your new outdoor gear to good use with a hike through the scenic **Wolfe's Neck Woods State Park**, where winding paths weave through pine and hemlock forests, and along the salt marshes and rocky shoreline of Casco Bay. End the day with a tasting at **Maine Beer Company**, known for its IPAs and craft brews.

Wiscasset Antiques Mall

WISCASSET

About 30 miles north along Route 1, you'll come to what is known as one of the prettiest villages in Maine: Wiscasset, home of the popular lobster roll spot **Red's Eats**. It lays claim to Maine's number-one lobster roll, but that's a hotly contested debate I don't care to enter! Perched on the Sheepscot River, the town has preserved the lovely historic churches and beautiful old homes that give this part of the country its unique charm. During the eighteenth and nineteenth centuries, Wiscasset prospered as a shipping port, which led to the building of grander homes, including the Nickels-Sortwell House, the Wood-Foote House, and the Governor Smith House. The town is known for its upscale antiques shops and art galleries; be sure to visit **Wiscasset Antiques Mall**; **Wiscasset Antiques Center**; the **Maine Art Gallery**, which features works by hundreds of local artists; and the elegant **Marston House**, known for impeccably sourced French antiques and textiles.

BOOTHBAY HARBOR

At this point, you've made your way through several coastal Maine towns, each with lighthouses and beaches aplenty. Boothbay Harbor has similar charms, but it is also home to **Coastal Maine Botanical Gardens**, New England's largest botanical garden—295 acres in all. Highlights include a rhododendron oasis with a cascading waterfall, ornamental display gardens, and walking trails through forests and hills and along the tidal Back River. Throughout the wooded areas, you'll come across five giant sculptures of trolls known as the Guardians of the Seeds (opposite). They were crafted from recycled wood by Thomas Dambo, a leading recycled-materials artist. Each troll imparts a different lesson centered on environmental stewardship. The gardens are a living museum of plants managed for conservation, research, and education.

Boothbay Harbor's downtown is small but packed with charming, independently owned shops. Be sure to stop by **Orne's Candy Store** and get some Needhams, a coconut and potato–filled chocolate that was invented in Maine, or save your sweet tooth for **Downeast Ice Cream Factory**.

As you head north on Route 1 toward Rockland, swing by **Moody's Diner** in Waldoboro, an iconic pit stop beloved for its humble vibe and scrumptious baked goods. Don't miss out on the whoopie pies and blueberry muffins.

Coastal Maine Botanical Gardens

ROCKLAND

It's hard not to love a tiny harbor town that holds the arts in such high esteem. Rockland has earned itself quite a reputation in the art world. Visit the **Wyeth Center at the Farnsworth Art Museum** to see paintings and sculptures by renowned American artists with Maine connections, most notably the Wyeths (N. C., Andrew, and James). And the **Center for Maine Contemporary Art** is known for works from emerging and established artists with ties to Maine.

To celebrate the Audubon Seabird Institute's success in bringing puffins and other rare Maine seabirds back to historic nesting islands, pay a visit to the **Project Puffin Visitor Center**, where you can see the birds in real time thanks to the innovative video system. Take a walk to the end of a long granite breakwater that juts out nearly a mile into the sea to visit the **Rockland Breakwater Lighthouse**, built in 1902.

Just 6 short miles from Rockland, swing through **Camden** and visit Maine's most well-known World War I memorial, the 26-foot-tall stone **Mount Battie Memorial Tower**, which was erected in 1921 on the summit of Mount Battie to recognize the services of men and women of Camden in the war. Afterward, cruise the historic district, comprising fifty-eight beautiful buildings on High Street between Main Street and Sherman Point Road.

Rockland Breakwater Lighthouse

BELFAST

Continue along Route 1 for about 18 miles until you reach Belfast, a delightful little city perched on a gentle hill above the Passagassawakeag River. The best way to see the town is the **Belfast In-Town Nature Trail**, a 5-mile loop that winds through tree-lined streets, city parks, birding hot spots and habitats for wildlife, and urban gardens. Continue your walking tour with the **Belfast Harbor Walk**, which is only about a mile long but offers stunning views of the harbor and surrounding islands.

Continue on foot by following the **Museum in the Streets** trail, an outdoor exhibit featuring thirty historical panels that tell the story of Belfast's past. You can take a self-guided tour of the exhibit and learn about the city's rich history, from its shipbuilding days to its role in the Civil War.

Additionally, walk or bike the **Belfast Rail Trail** on the Passagassawakeag, a 2.2-mile path that winds past vintage trains at one end and shipwrights at work at the other. The trail follows the southern section of old railbed laid by the **Belfast and Moosehead Lake Railroad**, a historic short line railroad that's been in operation for more than 150 years and still offers weekend round-trip excursions to Unity.

Common Ground Country Fair

Every fall, an estimated sixty thousand visitors converge on the small town of Unity—a half-hour drive inland from Belfast—to partake in the festivities of the Common Ground Country Fair. Touted as a three-day celebration of Maine's rich rural and agricultural history, the fair boasts a packed roster of activities, including music, speakers, exhibits, vendors, and demonstrations, all of which emphasize environmental sustainability, traditional craftsmanship, and organic farming. The Maine Organic Farmers and Gardeners Association, the oldest and largest state organic organization in the country, began hosting the fair in 1977, and the fair has grown steadily since.

Included on the extensive fairgrounds is the state's only all-organic farmers market, a large agricultural pavilion where Maine farmers demonstrate their working animals, and a fine art and craft area featuring the work of Maine artisans exclusively. At the food court, more than sixty vendors serve up delicacies ranging from lobster rolls and barbecue chicken to tofu scrambles and homemade ice cream, all prepared from Maine-sourced ingredients. More than seven hundred workshops, presentations, and demonstrations are held over the course of the three days, covering everything from organic gardening and agriculture to cooking, energy-efficient building, and environmental, health, and social issues.

Skip the traffic and the hunt for parking and take the Brooks Preservation Society train that runs directly to the fairgrounds from stations in Unity and Thorndike, or the aforementioned train from Belfast. Saturday and Sunday are the most jam-packed of the three days, so consider visiting on Friday for a less crowded experience.

BAR HARBOR

Bar Harbor is the perfect last stop in Maine. Plan to spend at least a few days exploring this charming town, and the real draw, **Acadia National Park**. Located primarily on Mount Desert Island, Acadia's 47,000 acres are a breathtaking landscape of forests, rocky beaches, and glacier-carved granite peaks, all of which provide an ample habitat for a diversity of wildlife.

Walk along the lovely coastal **Shore Path**, a great way to get the lay of the town. Stop in at the downtown Bar Harbor location of the **Abbe Museum**, which showcases the history and cultures of the Wabanaki people through exhibitions, special events, archaeology field schools, and workshops, and holds the largest collection of Maine Indian basketry. While in town, pay a visit to **Sherman's Maine Coast Book Shop**, the state's oldest bookstore, with nine locations across coastal Maine. The **George B. Dorr Museum of Natural History** is a wonderful place to learn about Maine's coastal wildlife through exhibits and living tide pools. The museum is housed in the original headquarters of Acadia National Park, which has been expanded and renovated.

Now it's time to head to Acadia National Park, where the hiking is spectacular, although there are also many scenic drives that provide amazing views. For a short hike, try the **Ocean Path** or the loop around **Jordan Pond** or **Echo Lake**. For the best sunrise views, get a predawn start and hike (or drive, though in summer you'll have to make a vehicle registration, such are the crowds) to the summit of **Cadillac Mountain**. Around the summit, there are hikes both long (the **South Ridge Trail**) and short (the **Cadillac Summit Loop**). Don't miss the stunning 110-foot-high **Otter Cliff** or nearby **Monument Cove**, a spot along the Ocean Path notable for the natural pillar of granite that resembles a monument (hence the name). Many of Acadia's most popular draws, including Sieur de Monts,

Sand Beach, Otter Point, Thunder Hole, Jordan Pond, and Cadillac Mountain, are located on Park Loop Road, a scenic 27-mile drive.

From Bar Harbor, you can easily grab a ferry to Nova Scotia (see page 180).

But it would be impossible to talk about New England without mentioning Vermont, the only state in New England that doesn't border the Atlantic Ocean.

Acadia National Park

Maine Islands

Looking to visit an island off the coast of Maine? There are plenty to choose from; in fact, there are more than four thousand! These rocky outcrops—and their hardy population of year-rounders—reflect Maine's independent character and are steeped in rich history. Here are just a few favorites:

Thief Island

Located in the Muscongus Bay, this is a great stop-off point for campers, kayakers, and boaters.

Monhegan Island

This small and rocky island doesn't have cars or paved roads, instead it offers a small village and nine miles of hiking trails.

Isle au Haut

One of the island's main draws is Acadia National Park, which covers approximately 60 percent of the island.

Casco Bay Islands

The Casco Bay contains more than 200 islands just offshore of Portland, accessible by ferries and the Mailboat.

Mount Desert Island

This is the largest island off the coast and is home to Acadia National Park and Bar Harbor.

Vinalhaven Island

Located in Penobscot Bay, Vinalhaven is both the name of the island and the town.

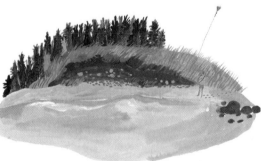

Matinicus Island

At 22 miles off the Gulf of Maine, this is the most remote of Maine's islands.

Deer Isle

Connected to the mainland via Deer Isle Bridge, this easily accessible island is home to the beautiful town of Stonington.

VERMONT

From the shores of Lake Champlain to the majestic peaks of the Green Mountains, road-tripping through Vermont offers a captivating journey through scenic landscapes, charming towns, and a rich tapestry of natural beauty. As you traverse the state, you'll be greeted by rolling green hills, bucolic farmland, meandering rivers, quaint villages with white-steepled churches, covered bridges, and farm stands offering fresh local goods, including the region's renowned maple syrup and artisanal cheeses. Whether during the vibrant fall leaf-peeping season, a winter wonderland, or the verdant beauty of summer, a road trip through Vermont is well worth the detour from the coast.

Québec
Lake Champlain
Mount Mansfield
Stowe
Burlington
New York
Henry Sheldon Museum
Vermont
Green Mountains
New Hampshire
Southern Vermont Arts Center
Manchester
Hildene, the Lincoln Family Home
Massachusetts

Start in Manchester, a historic former iron-mining hub tucked into the Green Mountains. Explore the town's boutiques, art galleries, and restaurants. Visit Hildene, the former home of Robert Todd Lincoln, the eldest son of President Abraham Lincoln and Mary Todd Lincoln, and take a tour of the Georgian Revival mansion and gardens. Nearby, the Southern Vermont Arts Center has a beautiful sculpture garden, wide-ranging exhibitions, and a performance space, plus sprawling grounds with forest pathways.

Southern Vermont Arts Center

Henry Sheldon Museum

From Manchester, head north on Route 7, which will take you through the scenic Champlain Valley. Enjoy pastoral views of rolling hills and farmland as you drive toward the town of Middlebury. Make a stop in Middlebury and take a stroll around the historic downtown area, visit the Henry Sheldon Museum of Vermont History, and wander through Middlebury College's stately campus.

Continue north to the town of Burlington, located on the eastern shore of Lake Champlain. Spend the evening exploring the vibrant downtown area, bustling with shops and excellent restaurants, and attractions like the Church Street Marketplace and ECHO, Leahy Center for Lake Champlain, a science and nature museum. Burlington is a great place to stop for the night.

Bluegill fish

Biking the Green Mountain State

Vermont is the ultimate playground for seriously fun cycling adventures, offering some of the best biking in the country. Hundreds of miles of trails connect Vermont towns, regions, and scenic vistas. Kingdom Trails stands out as a gem, offering a vast 100-mile network of trails weaving through northern Vermont. For those seeking an epic adventure, the famed LAMB (Lincoln, Appalachian, Middlebury, and Brandon Gaps) ride has you covered. This 100-mile pedal takes riders on a challenging journey across multiple passes and can be conquered in a single ambitious push, broken into out-and-back segments, or divided into enjoyable day rides.

For a different kind of thrill, Killington Ski Resort boasts world-class lift-accessed downhill mountain biking. The extensive trail system provides thrilling descents for riders of all levels, with varying terrains catering to both beginners and seasoned downhill bikers. If you're new to the sport, Killington is a great place to learn: Rent a bike from the ski area and take a lesson from one of the pros before hitting the slopes. The real win here: No need to bike uphill! Let the gondolas do the work for you!

In the town of Williston, the Catamount trails beckon with 20 miles of singletrack and doubletrack trails. This trail system offers a mix of technical sections and flowing pathways, making it a versatile choice for riders looking to test their skills or enjoy a leisurely ride through Vermont's beautiful countryside.

From Stowe, head northwest on VT 108, in part known as the Smugglers' Notch Scenic Highway. This route will take you through beautiful countryside, with stunning mountain views and charming small towns along the way. Stowe is an outdoorsy town, known for its trails and ski slopes. Hike or bike along the picturesque trails, or take a scenic gondola ride to the summit of Mount Mansfield, Vermont's highest peak. Visit Trapp Family Lodge, an Austrian-inspired mountain resort situated on 2,500 acres, run by the von Trapp family, whose story was the inspiration for *The Sound of Music*.

From Stowe, head northwest on VT 108, also known as the Smugglers' Notch Scenic Byway. This mountain road offers breathtaking views as it winds through a narrow pass between Mount Mansfield and Spruce Peak. Continue driving northwest to the town of St. Albans, located on the shores of Lake Champlain. Explore the downtown area, stroll along the waterfront, and visit the St. Albans Historical Museum to learn about the town's history. St Albans Bay Park offers a sandy beach and recreational activities along the lake. You can also take a scenic drive along Lake Champlain's shoreline.

Cheese Plate

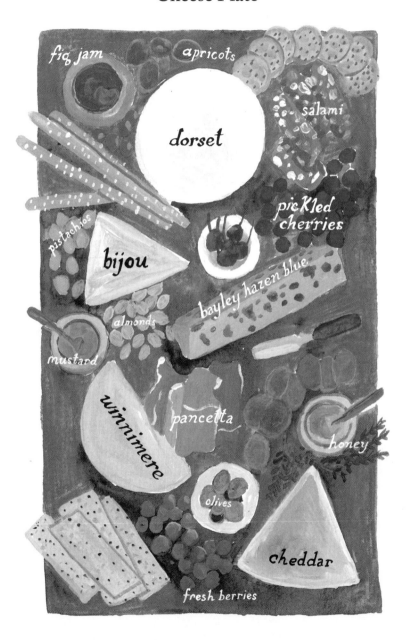

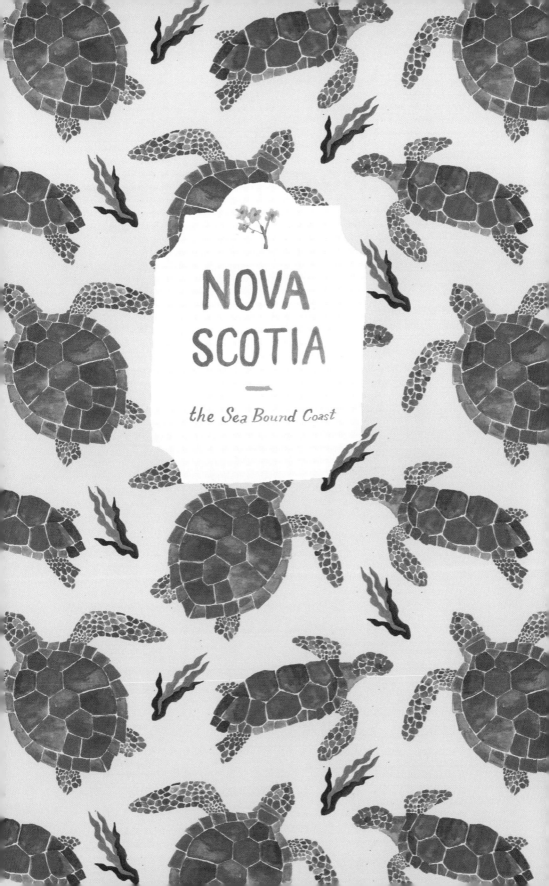

NOVA SCOTIA

the Sea Bound Coast

WELCOME TO
Nova Scotia

Did you pack your passport? We're heading north, over the Canadian border into Nova Scotia, the incredibly beautiful maritime province with more than 4,500 miles of coastline. If you make it this far, you'll be amply rewarded with breathtaking scenery, charming towns, and delicious seafood. It would take around eight hours to drive the entire length of the province, but that doesn't mean you should rush the journey. Weave along the sea around Canada's Ocean Playground to explore the coastal towns and villages, including Halifax, the province's buzzy capital city; Peggy's Cove, a delightful village famous for its lighthouse and rocky coastline; and Old Town Lunenburg, a UNESCO World Heritage Site with colorful historic buildings and a rich shipbuilding history. For those seeking outdoor adventures and wide-open vistas, this is a paradise. Take a kayak tour of Mahone Bay, or hit up the plentiful nature trails in Caledonia, where you'll get up close and personal with the region's abundant birdlife, including eagles, Atlantic puffins, loons, and great blue herons.

Begin your journey by catching the high-speed car ferry that travels between Bar Harbor, Maine, and Yarmouth, Nova Scotia, in just three and a half hours. From there, the coastal route is peppered with fascinating small towns. Here on the coast of Nova Scotia, Acadian history runs deep, dating back more than four hundred years. Europeans of French descent, attracted to the bounty of both the sea and the land, began colonizing Acadia, the area that is now New Brunswick, Nova Scotia, and Prince Edward Island, in the 1600s. Due to their amicable relations with the Native population, the Acadian people acquired the skills of hunting, fishing, and farming, which enabled them to thrive in the new land and establish their own unique customs, songs, and culture. During the French and Indian War, British officers forcefully deported around 11,500 Acadians because of their perceived alliance with the French. Acadians dispersed throughout North America and Europe. Once the war ended, they were able to return, and their culture continues to thrive today. To learn more about their fascinating history, make your way to the town of Pubnico and visit the Historic Acadian Village of Nova Scotia, the oldest Acadian settlement emulating pre-1920s Acadian life. Visit the blacksmith shop, fish sheds, and homes bearing their original architecture and period amenities, and don't miss the gift shop stocked with souvenirs made by local artisans.

Blacksmith at the
Historic Acadian Village
of Nova Scotia

Farther along the coast in Barrington, the Barrington Woolen Mill Museum harkens back to simpler times with demonstrations of hand spinning, dyeing, processing, and weaving. About half an hour away, the town of Shelburne boasts an artfully restored eighteenth-century historic district, complete with a dory shop, shipyard, and authentic general store. Visit Caledonia, home of Kejimkujik National Park, which spans 164.5 square miles of lakes, forests, and beaches and is steeped in Mi'kmaq heritage. In Cole Harbour, enjoy an afternoon at the Cole Harbour Heritage Farm Museum, which aims to preserve the town's agricultural traditions.

No visit to coastal Nova Scotia would be complete without a stop in the town of Digby, on the Bay of Fundy. The bay is home to the highest tides in the world, which can surpass the height of a five-story building, and its cold, deep waters create the ideal environment for fresh and delicious scallops, which Digby is known for. In 2020, the Cliffs of Fundy, located near Minas Basin in the Bay of Fundy, were granted the status of a UNESCO Global Geopark, making them the sixth UNESCO designation in the province. These magnificent cliffs formed by the high tides serve as a 300-million-year-old record of Pangea's history. This area holds a special attraction for fossil enthusiasts and great cultural significance for the Mi'kmaq people.

Finally, the historic town of Annapolis Royal offers a glimpse into Canada's colonial past, with its beautifully preserved architecture.

Annapolis Royal

There's an abundance of gorgeous gardens along the route, including the Annapolis Royal Historic Gardens; the Harriet Irving Botanical Gardens on the Acadia University campus; and Tangled Garden, both a delightful garden and a working farm that produces fresh herbs and fruits for its homemade jellies, liqueurs, vinegars, and cordials.

Nova Scotia has made it easy for roadtrippers with the Cabot Trail, a well-marked scenic loop that hugs the craggy coastline of Cape Breton Island and traverses the canyons and valleys of Cape Breton Highlands National Park. The winding 185-mile trail stretches from the sea to the mountains and blends highways, paths, stairs, and spectacular views as it takes you from breathtaking ocean vistas to quaint fishing villages.

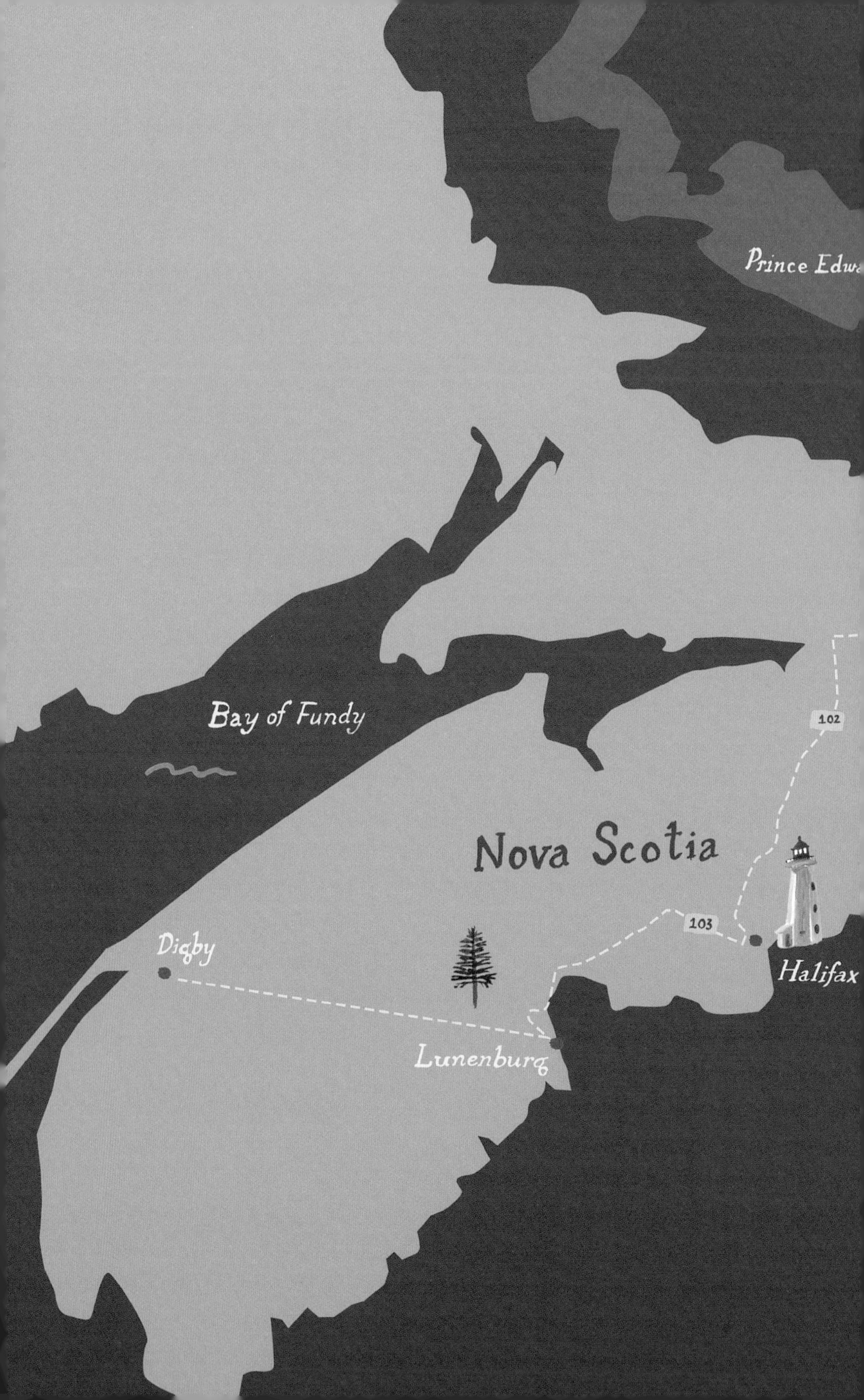

Prince Edwa

Bay of Fundy

Nova Scotia

102

103

Digby

Lunenburg

Halifax

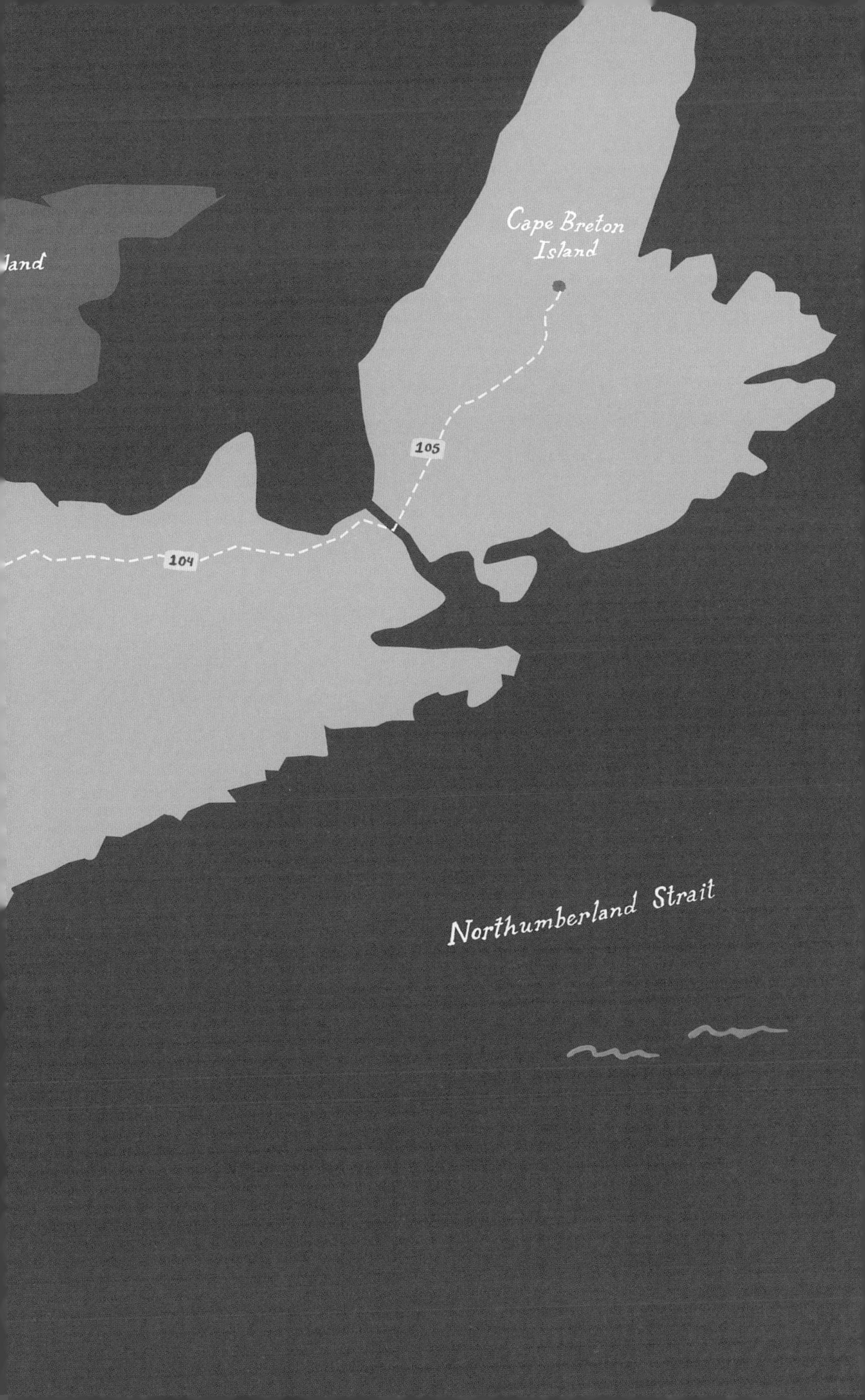

Cape Breton
Island

105

...land

104

Northumberland Strait

DESTINATIONS

Lunenburg
188

Halifax
191

Cape Breton Island
192

LUNENBURG

Your Nova Scotia journey most likely began when the ferry landed in Yarmouth. The roughly 140-mile drive from Yarmouth to Lunenburg takes a little over two hours straight, though I'd suggest leaving plenty of time to stop at some of the towns along the way.

Lunenburg is a UNESCO World Heritage Site, and more than 70 percent of the original eighteenth- and nineteenth-century colonial buildings still stand proud on the waterfront. Their colorful facades give the town a picture-perfect feel.

The **Fisheries Museum of the Atlantic**, where visitors can explore the town's seafaring past and learn about the local fishing industry, helps put the historic waterfront into context and lays bare the contrast between the beauty and romance of the sea and the harsh reality of making a living from it. The museum houses a wide range of exhibits, from historic boats and fishing gear to an aquarium showcasing marine life found in the region. Take a guided tour of the ***Bluenose II***, a replica of the famous Canadian schooner that was built in Lunenburg and became a national icon when it raced undefeated for the International Fishermen's Cup. The museum has three floors of exhibits, though the First Fishers Exhibit, told from the Mi'kmaq perspective, is especially enlightening.

Make time for a rum tasting at **Ironworks Distillery**, whose Rum Boat rum is specially crafted and aged in oak barrels both on land and at sea on a floating boat warehouse. And on your way out of town, just a few miles away, **Blue Rocks**, a working fishing village perched atop blue slate rocks, is a recommended stop.

The Little Painted House
of Maud Lewis

HALIFAX

Just over an hour from Lunenburg, Halifax, the capital of Nova Scotia, is a coastal metropolis that beautifully marries big-city culture with small-town friendliness. Stroll along the bustling waterfront lined with restaurants and shops, take a boat tour of the harbor, or explore the **Maritime Museum of the Atlantic**, which houses exhibits on Nova Scotia's illustrious seafaring history. With its strategic hilltop location, the **Halifax Citadel National Historic Site**, a star-shaped fortress with commanding views of the harbor, dates back to 1749 and offers immersive tours and exhibits highlighting the military history of the region. The **Halifax Public Gardens** are beautiful Victorian-era gardens filled with flowers, fountains, and statues.

The highlight of the **Art Gallery of Nova Scotia** is the largest public collection of works by beloved Nova Scotia folk artist Maud Lewis. She was known to paint everything—beach rocks, shells, household items. Even the inside and outside of her house is on display in the museum.

Head to the **Halifax Seaport Farmers' Market**, one of the oldest farmers markets in North America, first opened in 1750. You can sample local cheeses, meats, and fresh produce from the surrounding areas, as well as buy handmade crafts and artisanal goods. Its location offers beautiful views of Georges Island. Take a stroll through **Point Pleasant Park**, a sprawling park located on the southern tip of Halifax's peninsula. The park boasts impressive views of the ocean and the city, as well as walking trails, picnic areas, and a few small beaches.

One of the most iconic sights in Halifax is the **Peggy's Cove Lighthouse**, located just a short drive outside the city in St. Margarets Bay. The picturesque lighthouse is perched on top of rugged granite cliffs and offers breathtaking views of the Atlantic Ocean.

CAPE BRETON ISLAND

From Halifax, follow the Trans-Canada Highway for a little more than 200 miles to **Baddeck**, where the **Cabot Trail** begins. A world-renowned scenic drive that encircles Cape Breton Island, which sits at the eastern end of Nova Scotia, this 185-mile road trip offers remarkable views of the Atlantic Ocean, and encompasses the **Gulf of St. Lawrence**—known for migratory whales—and the rolling hills of the **Cape Breton Highlands National Park** at its northernmost point. Along the way, learn about the culture and customs of the Unama'ki (Cape Breton Island) five First Nation communities through stops at the **Mi'kmaw Interpretive Centre** and **Membertou Heritage Park**, where you can participate in a hand drum or beading workshop.

Head northeast from Baddeck, through Ingonish, to **Cape Breton Highlands National Park**, where the mountains meet the sea,

Cabot Trail

creating a lush landscape of old-growth forests and verdant river. The **Skyline Trail** footpath overlooks the Gulf of St. Lawrence and provides panoramic views of the coastal landscape. Farther along, after passing through Pleasant Bay, visit the fishing village of **Chéticamp**, an Acadian community whose rich history and culture are evident in its colorful buildings, traditional music, and delicious seafood. Sample some of the lobster, crab, and scallops that are harvested from the nearby waters. In addition to enjoying the fresh seafood, stop along the trail at one of the many roadside stands selling homemade jams, pies, and other treats made from local produce.

One of the highlights of driving the Cabot Trail is the opportunity to witness the changing colors of the landscape with the seasons. In fall, the trees burst into vibrant hues, creating a stunning backdrop for your road trip. In summer, the trail is lush and alive with the sounds of the ocean and the songs of migratory shorebirds. In winter, for those who brave the roads, the trail transforms into a winter wonderland, with snow-covered mountains and icy waterfalls.

Wildflowers
OF NOVA SCOTIA

Mayflower

Pitcher Plant

Harebell

Lupine

Rhodora

Forget-Me-Not

Wild Strawberry

Coltsfoot

Pin Cherry

BEFORE WE PART

"The land knows you, even when you are lost."

ROBIN WALL KIMMERER, *Braiding Sweetgrass*

As this winding journey concludes, my final hope is that wherever your path leads, you will encounter nature's wonders with deep respect. I hope you get lost, throw away the map, and chart your own course through this great and wonderful world. May you be motivated not only to explore and appreciate but also to safeguard the interconnected elements of our home—the ocean, the coast, the flora, the fauna, and the myriad creatures that inhabit the earth. It is crucial for us, as humans, to strike a harmonious balance within this intricate ecosystem we call home.

ROAD TRIP SCAVENGER HUNT

Keep your eyes peeled on your trip.
Can you find everything on this list?

☐ Camper

☐ Motorcycle

☐ Dog in a car

☐ Shaw's

☐ Bench

☐ Taxicab

☐ Person wearing sunglasses

☐ Someone sleeping in
a vehicle

☐ Rusty car

☐ Duct-taped car part

☐ Military vehicle

☐ Moose

☐ Purple car

☐ Horse

☐ The letter Q

☐ Someone eating in
a vehicle

☐ Market basket

☐ Grocery store

☐ Swan boats

☐ Christmas tree made of
lobster traps

☐ Sailboat

☐ Whale

☐ Railroad crossing

☐ Lobster roll

☐ 24/7 diner

☐ Ambulance

☐ Fluffernutter

☐ Church

☐ Someone walking a dog

☐ Tractor
☐ Colorful houses
☐ Barn
☐ Yellow car
☐ Gas station with no cars
☐ Statue
☐ Sports car
☐ Bird on a wire
☐ Water tower
☐ Canoe
☐ Arrow
☐ Green roof
☐ Train
☐ Bridge over water

☐ Flying kite
☐ Turtle
☐ Wedding party
☐ Cloud shaped like an animal
☐ Golf course
☐ Treehouse
☐ Umbrella
☐ Nest
☐ Jogger
☐ Feather
☐ Sand

CHRISTINE CHITNIS is a writer, a photographer, and the author of *Patterns of India* and *Patterns of Portugal*. As a contributor to publications including the *New York Times*, *Elle*, *Travel + Leisure*, and *Condé Nast Traveler*, Christine has earned a reputation as a multitalented storyteller. She lives in Providence, Rhode Island, with her husband and three children. Visit her at christinechitnis.com and follow her on Instagram at @christine.chitnis.

MONICA DORAZEWSKI is a freelance illustrator and graphic designer. She is also the illustrator of *The Snowy Cabin Cookbook*. Previous clients include Anthropologie, Terrain, Free People, Seedlings Greeting Cards, American Greetings, and Magnolia Journal. Monica finds inspiration in nature, travel, and flea markets. While a painting student at the Savannah College of Art and Design, she organically turned to graphic design and illustration as a means of artistic expression, and has since expanded her passions to include collage, sewing, and repeat pattern making. She currently resides in Ocean View, Delaware, with her husband and son. To see more of her work, visit monicadora.com and follow along on Instagram at @monicaedora.

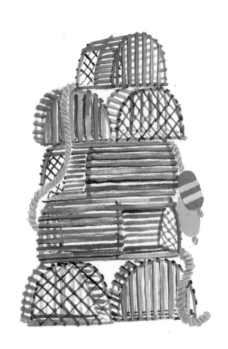